DOVER · THRIFT · EDITIONS

Great Sonnets

Edited by Paul Negri

DOVER PUBLICATIONS, INC.
New York

DOVER THRIFT EDITIONS

GENERAL EDITOR: STANLEY APPELBAUM

ACKNOWLEDGMENTS: see page xii.

Copyright

Published in Canada by General Publishing Company, Ltd., 30 Lesmill Road, Don Mills, Toronto, Ontario.
Published in the United Kingdom by Constable and Company, Ltd., 3 The Lanchesters, 162–164 Fulham Palace Road, London W6 9ER.

Bibliographical Note

Great Sonnets is a new anthology, first published by Dover Publications, Inc., in 1994.

Library of Congress Cataloging-in-Publication Data

Great sonnets / edited by Paul Negri.
    p.   cm. — (Dover thrift editions)
  ISBN 0-486-28052-7 (pbk.)
  1. Sonnets, English.   2. Sonnets, American.   I. Negri, Paul. II. Series.
PR1195.S5G74   1994
821'.04208 — dc20   94-6460
                                                      CIP

Manufactured in the United States of America
Dover Publications, Inc., 31 East 2nd Street, Mineola, N.Y. 11501

Note

Poets have been writing sonnets in English for more than 450 years. One of the oldest and most enduring poetic forms, the sonnet originated in Italy in the thirteenth century. The Italian poet Petrarch (1304–1374) established the definitive form of the sonnet, along with the idea of the sonnet sequence, a series of linked sonnets on a particular theme, usually love. During the Renaissance, a great revival of interest in the sonnet spread through many European countries.

The history of the sonnet in English begins with the courtier-poets Sir Thomas Wyatt and Henry Howard, Earl of Surrey, who introduced the sonnet form to England in the 1530s. In 1591 Sir Philip Sidney's great sonnet sequence *Astrophel and Stella* achieved enormous popularity and inaugurated a virtual sonnet craze in England that resulted in many of the best (and worst) sonnets ever written. From the mid-seventeenth through the mid-eighteenth centuries, the sonnet fell into a period of disuse, only to be revived again at the end of the eighteenth century, a revival that continues unabated to the present.

Technically, a sonnet is a fourteen-line poem usually in iambic pentameter (a line of some ten syllables basically alternating between unstressed and stressed)* and with a set rhyme scheme. There are two principal types, defined by their rhyme schemes: the English or Shakespearean sonnet and the Italian or Petrarchan sonnet. The English sonnet is composed of three quatrains (groups of four lines) and a

---

* In the Renaissance poems (Wyatt through Herbert) the meter of the line very often assumes a full pronunciation of "-ed" at the end of words. For example: "My galley charged with forgetfulness" (Wyatt, page 1). The line works metrically only if "charged" is given two syllables. Another example: "The sad account of fore-bemoaned moan" (Shakespeare, page 14).

concluding couplet (two lines), the most common rhyme scheme being abab cdcd efef gg. The Italian sonnet is divided into an octave (eight lines) and a sestet (six lines). The rhyme scheme of the octave is almost always abbaabba; the rhyme scheme of the sestet can vary. Many poets, however, have not allowed themselves to be restricted by rigid definitions of the sonnet and have used variations in rhyme and meter while retaining the essential sonnet form.

Included in this anthology are great sonnets by many of the greatest British and American poets and many fine sonnets by relatively minor poets as well. All have been selected for distinction in style or substance or both; and all display those essential qualities of the sonnet that have made it a favorite poetic form of poets and readers for centuries.

For the present edition, spelling in the older poems has been modernized.

Contents

Acknowledgments   xii

THOMAS WYATT (1503–1542)   1
    "The long love that in my thought doth harbor"
    "My galley charged with forgetfulness"
    "Farewell, love, and all thy laws forever"
    "Whoso list to hunt, I know where is an hind"

HENRY HOWARD, EARL OF SURREY (1517?–1547)   3
    The Soote Season
    "Love, that doth reign and live within my thought"

GEORGE GASCOIGNE (1525?–1577)   4
    "You must not wonder, though you think it strange"

SIR WALTER RALEGH (1552?–1618)   4
    [Sir Walter Ralegh to his Son]

EDMUND SPENSER (1552–1599)   5
    "Happy ye leaves! whenas those lily hands"
    "Most glorious Lord of life, that on this day"
    "One day I wrote her name upon the strand"
    "Fair is my love, when her fair golden hairs"

SIR PHILIP SIDNEY (1554–1586)   7
    "Loving in truth, and fain in verse my love to show"
    "With how sad steps, O Moon, thou climb'st the skies"
    "Come Sleep, O Sleep! the certain knot of peace"
    "Leave me, O Love, which reachest but to dust"

SAMUEL DANIEL (1562–1619)   9
    "Fair is my Love and cruel as she 's fair"
    "Care-charmer Sleep, son of the sable Night"
    "Let others sing of Knights and Paladines"
    "If this be love, to draw a weary breath"

MICHAEL DRAYTON (1563–1631)   11
    "Dear, why should you command me to my rest"
    "Since there's no help, come let us kiss and part"

JOSHUA SYLVESTER (1563–1618)   12
    "Were I as base as is the lowly plain"

WILLIAM SHAKESPEARE (1564–1616)   12
    "When I do count the clock that tells the time"
    "Shall I compare thee to a summer's day?"
    "When in disgrace with fortune and men's eyes"
    "When to the sessions of sweet silent thought"
    "Not marble, nor the gilded monuments"
    "Let me not to the marriage of true minds"
    "Th' expense of spirit in a waste of shame"
    "My mistress' eyes are nothing like the sun"

BARNABE BARNES (1569?–1609)   16
    "Ah, sweet Content, where is thy mild abode?"

JOHN DONNE (1573–1631)   17
    "Thou hast made me, and shall thy work decay?"
    "At the round earth's imagin'd corners, blow"
    "Death be not proud, though some have called thee"
    "Batter my heart, three-person'd God; for you"

WILLIAM DRUMMOND OF HAWTHORNDEN (1585–1649)   19
    "I know that all beneath the moon decays"
    "My lute, be as thou wert when thou didst grow"

GEORGE HERBERT (1593–1633)   20
    Prayer
    Redemption

JOHN MILTON (1608–1674)   21
    On His Being Arrived to the Age of Twenty-Three
    On His Blindness
    On the Late Massacre in Piedmont
    On His Deceased Wife
    To the Lord General Cromwell, on the Proposals of Certain
        Ministers at the Committee for the Propagation of the Gospel

THOMAS GRAY (1716–1771)   23
    On the Death of Mr. Richard West

WILLIAM BLAKE (1757–1827)   24
    To the Evening Star

ROBERT BURNS (1759–1796)   24
    A Sonnet upon Sonnets

WILLIAM LISLE BOWLES (1762–1850)   25
    "O Time! who know'st a lenient hand to lay"

WILLIAM WORDSWORTH (1770–1850)   25
    "Nuns fret not at their convent's narrow room"
    Scorn Not the Sonnet
    "It is a beauteous evening, calm and free"
    "Surprised by joy — impatient as the wind"
    Composed Upon Westminster Bridge, September 3, 1802
    "The world is too much with us; late and soon"

SAMUEL TAYLOR COLERIDGE (1772–1834)   28
    Work Without Hope
    On a Discovery Made Too Late

ROBERT SOUTHEY (1774–1843)   29
    Winter

CHARLES LAMB (1775–1834)   30
    "A timid grace sits trembling in her eye"

JOSEPH BLANCO WHITE (1775–1841)   30
    To Night

LEIGH HUNT (1784–1859)   31
    The Nile
    To the Grasshopper and the Cricket

GEORGE GORDON, LORD BYRON (1788–1824)   32
    Sonnet on Chillon

PERCY BYSSHE SHELLEY (1792–1822)   32
    Ozymandias
    Sonnet: England in 1819
    "Lift not the painted veil which those who live"

WILLIAM CULLEN BRYANT (1794–1878)   34
    Midsummer
    November

JOHN KEATS (1795–1821)   35
    On First Looking into Chapman's Homer
    On Sitting Down to Read *King Lear* Once Again
    On Seeing the Elgin Marbles
    "Why did I laugh to-night? No voice will tell"
    When I Have Fears
    Bright Star

HARTLEY COLERIDGE (1796–1849)   38
    Prayer
    "Long time a child, and still a child, when years"

THOMAS HOOD (1799–1845)   39
    Silence
    Death

ELIZABETH BARRETT BROWNING (1806–1861)   40
    "If thou must love me, let it be for nought"
    "Belovèd, my Belovèd, when I think"
    "If I leave all for thee, wilt thou exchange"
    "How do I love thee? Let me count the ways"

HENRY WADSWORTH LONGFELLOW (1807–1882)   42
    Mezzo Cammin
    The Cross of Snow
    Milton
    The Poets

JOHN GREENLEAF WHITTIER (1807–1892)   44
    Forgiveness
    Godspeed

CHARLES TENNYSON TURNER (1808–1879)   45
    The Buoy-Bell
    Orion

ALFRED, LORD TENNYSON (1809–1892)   46
    "If I were loved, as I desire to be"
    Poets and Their Bibliographies

EDGAR ALLAN POE (1809–1849)   47
    To Science
    Silence

WILLIAM BELL SCOTT (1811–1890)   48
    My Mother
    A Garland for Advancing Years

JONES VERY (1813–1880)   49
    The Columbine
    The Fair Morning
    The Clouded Morning

JAMES RUSSELL LOWELL (1819–1891)   50
    The Street

FREDERICK GODDARD TUCKERMAN (1821–1873)   51
    "An upper chamber in a darkened house"
    "Last night I dreamed we parted once again"

MATTHEW ARNOLD (1822–1888)   52
    Shakespeare
    West London

GEORGE MEREDITH (1828–1909)   53
    Lucifer in Starlight
    "By this he knew she wept with waking eyes"
    "In our old shipwrecked days there was an hour"
    "Thus piteously Love closed what he begat"

DANTE GABRIEL ROSSETTI (1828–1882)   55
    A Sonnet
    Silent Noon
    A Superscription
    The One Hope

CHRISTINA ROSSETTI (1830–1894)   57
    Rest
    Youth Gone
    After Death
    Remember

THEODORE WATTS-DUNTON (1832–1914)   59
    The Sonnet's Voice
    Coleridge

WILLIAM MORRIS (1834–1896)   60
    Summer Dawn

ALGERNON CHARLES SWINBURNE (1837–1909)   60
    Love and Sleep

JOHN ADDINGTON SYMONDS (1840–1893)   61
    The Sonnet (III)
    Lux Est Umbra Dei

WILFRID SCAWEN BLUNT (1840–1922)   62
    On Her Vanity
    As to His Choice of Her
    To One Who Would Make a Confession

THOMAS HARDY (1840–1928)   63
    Hap
    Often When Warring

MATHILDE BLIND (1841–1896)   64
    The Dead

EDWARD DOWDEN (1843–1913)   65
    Leonardo's "Mona Lisa"
    Two Infinities

ROBERT BRIDGES (1844–1930)   66
    "While yet we wait for spring, and from the dry"
    "In autumn moonlight, when the white air wan"

GERARD MANLEY HOPKINS (1844–1889)   67
    God's Grandeur
    Spring
    [Carrion Comfort]
    "No worst, there is none. Pitched past pitch of grief"

EUGENE LEE-HAMILTON (1845–1907)   69
    What the Sonnet Is
    Sunken Gold

ALICE MEYNELL (1847–1922)   70
    Renouncement
    Changeless

EMMA LAZARUS (1849–1887)   71
    The New Colossus
    Echoes

JAMES WHITCOMB RILEY (1849–1916)   72
    Silence
    Eternity

PHILIP BOURKE MARSTON (1850–1887)   73
    Love's Music
    A Vain Wish

OSCAR WILDE (1856–1900)   74
    Hélas
    E Tenebris

CHARLES G. D. ROBERTS (1860–1943)   75
    Burnt Lands
    The Night Sky

WILLIAM BUTLER YEATS (1865–1939)   76
    Leda and the Swan
    Meru

ERNEST DOWSON (1867–1900)   77
    To One in Bedlam
    A Last Word

EDWIN ARLINGTON ROBINSON (1869–1935)   78
    Reuben Bright
    How Annandale Went Out

LORD ALFRED DOUGLAS (1870–1945)   79
    The Dead Poet
    To Sleep

PAUL LAURENCE DUNBAR (1872–1906)   80
    Douglass
    Slow Through the Dark

ROBERT FROST (1875–1963)   81
    Once by the Pacific
    Acquainted with the Night
    The Oven Bird
    Acceptance

SIEGFRIED SASSOON (1886–1967)   83
    Dreamers

RUPERT BROOKE (1887–1915)   83
    The Soldier

EDNA ST. VINCENT MILLAY (1892–1950)   84
    "Oh, sleep forever in the Latmian cave"
    "Love is not all: it is not meat nor drink"
    "What lips my lips have kissed, and where, and why"
    "Euclid alone has looked on Beauty bare"

ARCHIBALD MACLEISH (1892–1982)   86
    The End of the World

WILFRED OWEN (1893–1918)   86
    Anthem for Doomed Youth
    On Seeing a Piece of Our Artillery Brought into Action

Alphabetical List of Titles and First Lines   89

Acknowledgments

"The Oven Bird," "Acceptance," "Acquainted with the Night" and "Once by the Pacific" from *The Poetry of Robert Frost*, edited by Edward Connery Lathem. Copyright © 1956 by Robert Frost. Copyright 1916, 1928, 1930, 1939, 1949, © 1969 by Henry Holt and Company, Inc. Reprinted by permission of Henry Holt and Company, Inc.

The selection of poems by Robert Frost in this volume is published in the British Commonwealth by permission of the Estate of the author, and Edward Connery Latham, editor of *The Poetry of Robert Frost*, published by Jonathan Cape, Ltd., London.

"The End of the World" from *Collected Poems 1917–1982* by Archibald MacLeish. Copyright © 1985 by the Estate of Archibald MacLeish. Reprinted by permission of Houghton Mifflin Co. All rights reserved.

"Oh, sleep forever in the Latmian cave," "Love is not all: it is not meat or drink," "What lips my lips have kissed, and where, and why" and "Euclid alone has looked on beauty bare" from *Collected Poems* by Edna St. Vincent Millay, Harper & Row. Copyright © 1923, 1931, 1951, 1958 by Edna St. Vincent Millay and Norma Millay Ellis. Reprinted by permission of Elizabeth Barnett, literary executor.

"Anthem for Doomed Youth" and "On Seeing a Piece of Our Artillery Brought into Action" from *Collected Poems of Wilfred Owen*. Copyright © 1964 by Chatto & Windus, Ltd. Reprinted by permission of New Directions Publishing Corp.

"Dreamers" from *Collected Poems 1908–1956* by Siegfried Sassoon. Reprinted by permission of George Sassoon.

"An upper chamber in a darkened house" and "Last night I dreamed we parted once again" from *The Complete Poems of Frederick Goddard Tuckerman*, by N. Scott Momaday and Frederick Goddard Tuckerman.

SIR THOMAS WYATT *(1503–1542)*

POET AND courtier active in the service of Henry VIII. Through his adaptations of
Petrarch, he introduced the sonnet form to England in the 1530s.

"The long love that in my thought doth harbor"

The long love that in my thought doth harbor,
And in mine heart doth keep his residence,
Into my face presseth with bold pretense,
And there campeth, displaying his banner.
She that me learneth to love and to suffer,
And wills that my trust and lust's negligence
Be reined by reason, shame, and reverence,
With his hardiness taketh displeasure.
Wherewith love to the heart's forest he fleeth,
Leaving his enterprise with pain and cry,
And there him hideth and not appeareth.
What may I do when my master feareth
    But in the field with him to live and die?
    For good is the life ending faithfully.

"My galley charged with forgetfulness"

My galley charged with forgetfulness
Through sharp seas in winter nights doth pass
Tween rock and rock, and eke[1] my foe (alas)
That is my lord, steereth with cruelness.
And every oar, a thought in readiness,
As though that death were light in such a case;
An endless wind doth tear the sail apace
Of forced sighs and trusty fearfulness;
A rain of tears, a cloud of dark disdain,
Have done the wearied cords great hinderance;
Wreathed with error and eke with ignorance,
The stars be hid that led me to this pain.
    Drowned is reason that should be my comfort,
    And I remain, despairing of the port.

---

[1] [Also.]

"Farewell, love, and all thy laws forever"

Farewell, love, and all thy laws forever,
Thy baited hooks shall tangle me no more:
Senec and Plato call me from thy lore
To perfect wealth, my wit for to endeavor.
In blind error when I did persever,
Thy sharp repulse that pricketh aye so sore
Taught me in trifles that I set no store,
But scape forth, since liberty is lever.[1]
Therefore, farewell, go trouble younger hearts,
And in me claim no more authority;
With idle youth go use thy property,
And thereon spend thy many brittle darts.
   For hitherto though I have lost my time,
   Me list[2] no longer rotten boughs to climb.

"Whoso list to hunt, I know where is an hind"

Whoso list[3] to hunt, I know where is an hind,
But as for me, alas, I may no more,
The vain travail hath wearied me so sore.
I am of them that farthest cometh behind;
Yet may I by no means my wearied mind
Draw from the Deer: but as she fleeth afore,
Fainting I follow. I leave off therefore,
Since in a net I seek to hold the wind.
Who list her hunt, I put him out of doubt,
As well as I may spend his time in vain:
And, graven with diamonds, in letters plain
There is written her fair neck round about:
   Noli me tangere,[4] for Caesar's I am;
   And wild for to hold, though I seem tame.

---

[1] [Dearer.]
[2] [I want.]
[3] [Should desire.]
[4] [*Touch me not.*]

HENRY HOWARD, EARL OF SURREY (1517?–1547)

FRIEND OF Wyatt, with whom he shares credit for introducing the sonnet form to England. He was accused of treason by Henry VIII and executed.

The Soote Season

The soote[1] season, that bud and bloom forth brings,
With green hath clad the hill and eke the vale;
The nightingale with feathers new she sings;
The turtle to her mate hath told her tale.
Summer is come, for every spray now springs,
The hart hath hung his old head on the pale;
The buck in brake[2] his winter coat he flings;
The fishes flete[3] with new repairèd scale;
The adder all her slough away she slings;
The swift swallow pursueth the flyes smale;
The busy bee her honey now she mings,[4]
Winter is worn that was the flowers' bale.
  And thus I see among these pleasant things
  Each care decays, and yet my sorrow springs.

"Love, that doth reign and live within my thought"

Love, that doth reign and live within my thought
And build his seat within my captive breast,
Clad in arms wherein with me he fought,
Oft in my face he doth his banner rest.
But she that taught me love and suffer pain,
My doubtful hope and eke my hot desire
With shamefast look to shadow and refrain,
Her smiling grace converteth straight to ire.
And coward Love, then, to the heart apace
Taketh his flight, where he doth lurk and 'plain,
His purpose lost, and dare not show his face.
For my lord's guilt thus faultless bide I pain,
  Yet from my lord shall not my foot remove:
  Sweet is the death that taketh end by love.

---

[1] [Sweet.]
[2] [Thicket.]
[3] [Float.]
[4] [Mingles.]

GEORGE GASCOIGNE *(1525?–1577)*

DRAMATIST AND poet, Gascoigne is credited with having written the earliest English critical essay on the writing of poetry.

"You must not wonder, though you think it strange"

You must not wonder, though you think it strange,
To see me hold my lowering head so low;
And that mine eyes take no delight to range
About the gleams which on your face do grow.
The mouse which once hath broken out of trap
Is seldom teased with the trustless bait,
But lies aloof for fear of more mishap,
And feedeth still in doubt of deep deceit.
The scorched fly which once hath 'scap'd the flame
Will hardly come to play again with fire.
Whereby I learn that grievous is the game
Which follows fancy dazzled by desire.
    So that I wink or else hold down my head,
    Because your blazing eyes my bale have bred.

SIR WALTER RALEGH *(1552?–1618)*

POET, SOLDIER and courtier, favorite of Queen Elizabeth. Declining political fortunes resulted in long imprisonment in the Tower of London and his eventual execution by James I.

[Sir Walter Ralegh to his Son]

Three things there be that prosper up apace
And flourish, whilst they grow asunder far,
But on a day, they meet all in one place,
And when they meet, they one another mar;
And they be these: the wood, the weed, the wag.
The wood is that which makes the gallow tree;
The weed is that which strings the hangman's bag;
The wag, my pretty knave, betokeneth thee.
Mark well, dear boy, whilst these assemble not,
Green springs the tree, hemp grows, the wag is wild,
But when they meet, it makes the timber rot;
It frets the halter, and it chokes the child.
    Then bless thee, and beware, and let us pray
    We part not with thee at this meeting day.

EDMUND SPENSER (1552–1599)

AUTHOR OF *The Faerie Queene*. The sonnets presented here are from his *Amoretti*, a sequence of 88 sonnets.

"Happy ye leaves! whenas those lily hands"

Happy ye leaves! whenas those lily hands,
Which hold my life in their dead doing might,
Shall handle you, and hold in love's soft bands,
Like captives trembling at the victor's sight.
And happy lines! on which, with starry light,
Those lamping eyes will deign sometimes to look,
And read the sorrows of my dying sprite,
Written with tears in heart's close bleeding book.
And happy rhymes! bathed in the sacred brook
Of Helicon, whence she derived is,
When ye behold that angel's blessed look,
My soul's long lacked food, my heaven's bliss.
   Leaves, lines, and rhymes seek her to please alone,
   Whom if ye please, I care for other none.

"Most glorious Lord of life, that on this day"

Most glorious Lord of life, that on this day
Didst make thy triumph over death and sin,
And having harrowed hell, didst bring away
Captivity thence captive, us to win:
This joyous day, dear Lord, with joy begin,
And grant that we, for whom thou diddest die,
Being with thy dear blood clean washed from sin,
May live forever in felicity:
And that thy love we weighing worthily,
May likewise love thee for the same again;
And for thy sake, that all like dear didst buy,
May love with one another entertain.
   So let us love, dear love, like as we ought,
   Love is the lesson which the Lord us taught.

"One day I wrote her name upon the strand"

One day I wrote her name upon the strand,
But came the waves and washed it away:
Again I wrote it with a second hand,
But came the tide, and made my pains his prey.
Vain man, said she, that dost in vain assay
A mortal thing so to immortalize!
For I myself shall like to this decay,
And eek[1] my name be wiped out likewise.
Not so (quoth I), let baser things devise
To die in dust, but you shall live by fame:
My verse your virtues rare shall eternize,
And in the heavens write your glorious name;
    Where, whenas death shall all the world subdue,
    Our love shall live, and later life renew.

"Fair is my love, when her fair golden hairs"

Fair is my love, when her fair golden hairs
With the loose wind ye waving chance to mark:
Fair, when the rose in her red cheeks appears,
Or in her eyes the fire of love does spark:
Fair, when her breast, like a rich laden bark
With precious merchandise she forth doth lay:
Fair, when that cloud of pride, which oft doth dark
Her goodly light, with smiles she drives away—
But fairest she, when so she doth display
The gate with pearls and rubies richly dight,[2]
Through which her words so wise do make their way,
To bear the message of her gentle sprite.
    The rest be works of Nature's wonderment,
    But this the work of heart's astonishment.

---

[1] [Also.]
[2] [Arranged.]

SIR PHILIP SIDNEY *(1554–1586)*

SIDNEY'S GREAT sonnet sequence *Astrophel and Stella* (published in 1591), from which the first three selections are taken, was enormously popular and influential, inaugurating the great vogue for sonnet sequences in the 1590s.

"Loving in truth, and fain in verse my love to show"

Loving in truth, and fain in verse my love to show,
That the dear she might take some pleasure of my pain,
Pleasure might cause her read, reading might make her know,
Knowledge might pity win, and pity grace obtain,
I sought fit words to paint the blackest face of woe:
Studying inventions fine, her wits to entertain,
Oft turning others' leaves, to see if thence would flow
Some fresh and fruitful showers upon my sunburned brain.
But words came halting forth, wanting Invention's stay;
Invention, Nature's child, fled stepdame Study's blows;
And others' feet still seemed but strangers in my way.
Thus, great with child to speak, and helpless in my throes,
Biting my truant pen, beating myself for spite:
"Fool," said my Muse to me, "look in thy heart, and write."

"With how sad steps, O Moon, thou climb'st the skies!"

With how sad steps, O Moon, thou climb'st the skies!
How silently, and with how wan a face!
What! may it be that even in heavenly place
That busy archer his sharp arrows tries?
Sure, if that long-with-love-acquainted eyes
Can judge of love, thou feel'st a lover's case:
I read it in thy looks; thy languish'd grace
To me, that feel the like, thy state descries.
Then, even of fellowship, O Moon, tell me,
Is constant love deem'd there but want of wit?
Are beauties there as proud as here they be?
Do they above love to be loved, and yet
Those lovers scorn whom that love doth possess?
Do they call "virtue" there — ungratefulness?

"Come, Sleep, O Sleep! the certain knot of peace"

Come, Sleep, O Sleep! the certain knot of peace,
The baiting place of wit, the balm of woe,
The poor man's wealth, the prisoner's release,
Th' indifferent judge between the high and low;
With shield of proof shield me from out the prease[1]
Of those fierce darts despair at me doth throw:
O make in me those civil wars to cease;
I will good tribute pay, if thou do so.
Take thou of me smooth pillows, sweetest bed,
A chamber deaf to noise and blind to light,
A rosy garland, and a weary head:
And if these things, as being thine by right,
    Move not thy heavy grace, thou shalt in me,
    Livelier than elsewhere, Stella's image see.

"Leave me, O Love, which reachest but to dust"

Leave me, O Love, which reachest but to dust;
And thou, my mind, aspire to higher things;
Grow rich in that which never taketh rust;
Whatever fades, but fading pleasure brings.
Draw in thy beams, and humble all thy might
To that sweet yoke where lasting freedoms be,
Which breaks the clouds and opens forth the light,
That doth both shine and give us light to see.
O take fast hold; let that light be thy guide
In this small course which birth draws out to death,
And think how evil becometh him to slide
Who seeketh heaven, and comes of heavenly breath.
    Then farewell, world; thy uttermost I see:
    Eternal Love, maintain thy life in me.

---

[1] [Press.]

SAMUEL DANIEL *(1562–1619)*

POET, ESSAYIST and writer. The sonnets here are from his sequence *Delia* (published in 1592).

"Fair is my Love and cruel as she's fair"

Fair is my Love and cruel as she's fair;
Her brow-shades frown, although her eyes are sunny.
Her smiles are lightning, though her pride despair,
And her disdains are gall, her favours honey:
A modest maid, deck'd with a blush of honour,
Whose feet do tread green paths of youth and love;
The wonder of all eyes that look upon her,
Sacred on earth, design'd a Saint above.
Chastity and Beauty, which were deadly foes,
Live reconcilèd friends within her brow;
And had she Pity to conjoin with those,
Then who had heard the plaints I utter now?
    For had she not been fair, and thus unkind,
    My Muse had slept, and none had known my mind.

"Care-charmer Sleep, son of the sable Night"

Care-charmer Sleep, son of the sable Night,
Brother to Death, in silent darkness born,
Relieve my languish, and restore the light;
With dark forgetting of my care return;
And let the day be time enough to mourn
The shipwreck of my ill-adventured youth:
Let waking eyes suffice to wail their scorn,
Without the torment of the night's untruth.
Cease, dreams, the images of day-desires,
To model forth the passions of the morrow;
Never let rising sun approve you liars,
To add more grief to aggravate my sorrow.
    Still let me sleep, embracing clouds in vain,
    And never wake to feel the day's disdain.

"Let others sing of Knights and Paladines"

Let others sing of Knights and Paladines,
In aged accents and untimely words,
Paint shadows in imaginary lines,
Which well the reach of their high wit records.
But I must sing of thee, and those fair eyes
Authentic shall my verse in time to come,
When yet th' unborn shall say, Lo, where she lies!
Whose beauty made him speak, that else was dumb!
These are the arcs, the trophies I erect,
That fortify thy name against old age;
And these thy sacred virtues must protect
Against the Dark and Time's consuming rage.
    Though th' error of my youth in them appear,
    Suffice, they show I lived, and loved thee dear.

"If this be love, to draw a weary breath"

If this be love, to draw a weary breath,
To paint on floods till the shore cry to th' air,
With downward looks, still reading on the earth
The sad memorials of my love's despair;
If this be love, to war against my soul,
Lie down to wail, rise up to sigh and grieve,
The never-resting stone of care to roll,
Still to complain my griefs whilst none relieve;
If this be love, to clothe me with dark thoughts,
Haunting untrodden paths to wail apart;
My pleasures horror, music tragic notes,
Tears in mine eyes and sorrow at my heart.
    If this be love, to live a living death,
    Then do I love and draw this weary breath.

MICHAEL DRAYTON (1563–1631)

PROLIFIC WRITER of sonnets, odes, satires, religious and other verse. The following sonnets are from his 1619 sequence *Idea*.

"Dear, why should you command me to my rest"

Dear, why should you command me to my rest,
When now the night doth summon all to sleep?
Methinks this time becometh lovers best:
Night was ordained together friends to keep.
How happy are all other living things,
Which though the day disjoin by several flight,
The quiet Evening yet together brings,
And each returns unto his love at night!
O thou that art so courteous unto all,
Why shouldst thou, Night, abuse me only thus,
That every creature to his kind dost call,
And yet 'tis thou dost only sever us?
      Well could I wish it would be ever day,
      If, when night comes, you bid me go away.

"Since there's no help, come let us kiss and part"

Since there's no help, come let us kiss and part, —
Nay I have done, you get no more of me;
And I am glad, yea, glad with all my heart,
That thus so cleanly I myself can free;
Shake hands for ever, cancel all our vows,
And when we meet at any time again,
Be it not seen in either of our brows
That we one jot of former love retain.
Now at the last gasp of love's latest breath,
When his pulse failing, passion speechless lies,
When faith is kneeling by his bed of death,
And innocence is closing up his eyes,
      — Now if thou would'st, when all have given him over,
      From death to life thou might'st him yet recover!

JOSHUA SYLVESTER (1563–1618)

POET AND translator, Sylvester is remembered principally for his translation of the French poet Du Bartas' *Les Semaines*.

"Were I as base as is the lowly plain"

Were I as base as is the lowly plain,
And you, my Love, as high as heaven above,
Yet should the thoughts of me your humble swain
Ascend to heaven, in honour of my Love.
Were I as high as heaven above the plain,
And you, my Love, as humble and as low
As are the deepest bottoms of the main,
Whereso'er you were, with you my love should go.
Were you the earth, dear Love, and I the skies,
My love should shine on you like to the sun,
And look upon you with ten thousand eyes
Till heaven wax'd blind, and till the world were done.
    Whereso'er I am, below, or else above you,
    Whereso'er you are, my heart shall truly love you.

WILLIAM SHAKESPEARE (1564–1616)

SHAKESPEARE'S SONNET sequence of 154 poems was published in 1609 and includes what are generally considered to be the greatest sonnets in English.

"When I do count the clock that tells the time"

When I do count the clock that tells the time,
And see the brave day sunk in hideous night;
When I behold the violet past prime,
And sable curls, all silver'd o'er with white;
When lofty trees I see barren of leaves,
Which erst from heat did canopy the herd,
And summer's green all girded up in sheaves,
Borne on the bier with white and bristly beard;
Then of thy beauty do I question make,
That thou among the wastes of time must go,
Since sweets and beauties do themselves forsake,
And die as fast as they see others grow;
    And nothing 'gainst Time's scythe can make defence
    Save breed, to brave him when he takes thee hence.

"Shall I compare thee to a summer's day?"

Shall I compare thee to a summer's day?
Thou art more lovely and more temperate:
Rough winds do shake the darling buds of May,
And summer's lease hath all too short a date:
Sometime too hot the eye of heaven shines,
And often is his gold complexion dimm'd;
And every fair from fair sometime declines,
By chance, or nature's changing course, untrimm'd;
But thy eternal summer shall not fade,
Nor lose possession of that fair thou owest;
Nor shall Death brag thou wander'st in his shade,
When in eternal lines to time thou growest;
    So long as men can breathe, or eyes can see,
    So long lives this, and this gives life to thee.

"When in disgrace with fortune and men's eyes"

When in disgrace with fortune and men's eyes,
I all alone beweep my outcast state,
And trouble deaf Heaven with my bootless cries,
And look upon myself, and curse my fate,
Wishing me like to one more rich in hope,
Featur'd like him, like him with friends possess'd,
Desiring this man's art, and that man's scope,
With what I most enjoy contented least;
Yet in these thoughts myself almost despising,
Haply I think on thee, — and then my state
(Like to the lark at break of day arising
From sullen earth) sings hymns at heaven's gate;
    For thy sweet love remember'd such wealth brings,
    That then I scorn to change my state with kings'.

"When to the sessions of sweet silent thought"

When to the sessions of sweet silent thought
I summon up remembrance of things past,
I sigh the lack of many a thing I sought,
And with old woes new wail my dear time's waste:
Then can I drown an eye, unus'd to flow,
For precious friends hid in death's dateless night,
And weep afresh love's long-since cancell'd woe,
And moan the expense of many a vanish'd sight.
Then can I grieve at grievances foregone,
And heavily from woe to woe tell o'er
The sad account of fore-bemoaned moan,
Which I new pay as if not paid before.
    But if the while I think on thee, dear friend,
    All losses are restor'd, and sorrows end.

"Not marble, nor the gilded monuments"

Not marble, nor the gilded monuments
Of princes, shall outlive this powerful rhyme;
But you shall shine more bright in these contents
Than unswept stone, besmear'd with sluttish time.
When wasteful war shall statues overturn,
And broils root out the work of masonry,
Nor Mars his sword nor war's quick fire shall burn
The living record of your memory.
'Gainst death and all-oblivious enmity
Shall you pace forth; your praise shall still find room,
Even in the eyes of all posterity
That wear this world out to the ending doom.
    So, till the judgment that yourself arise,
    You live in this, and dwell in lovers' eyes.

"Let me not to the marriage of true minds"

Let me not to the marriage of true minds
Admit impediments. Love is not love
Which alters when it alteration finds,
Or bends with the remover to remove:
O no; it is an ever-fixed mark,
That looks on tempests, and is never shaken;
It is the star to every wandering bark,
Whose worth's unknown, although his height be taken.
Love's not Time's fool, though rosy lips and cheeks
Within his bending sickle's compass come;
Love alters not with his brief hours and weeks,
But bears it out even to the edge of doom.
   If this be error, and upon me prov'd,
   I never writ, nor no man ever lov'd.

"Th' expense of spirit in a waste of shame"

Th' expense of spirit in a waste of shame
Is lust in action; and till action, lust
Is perjur'd, murderous, bloody, full of blame,
Savage, extreme, rude, cruel, not to trust;
Enjoy'd no sooner, but despised straight;
Past reason hunted; and no sooner had,
Past reason hated, as a swallow'd bait,
On purpose laid to make the taker mad:
Mad in pursuit, and in possession so;
Had, having, and in quest to have, extreme;
A bliss in proof, — and prov'd, a very woe;
Before, a joy propos'd; behind, a dream:
   All this the world well knows; yet none knows well
   To shun the heaven that leads men to this hell.

"My mistress' eyes are nothing like the sun"

My mistress' eyes are nothing like the sun;
Coral is far more red than her lips' red:
If snow be white, why then her breasts are dun;
If hairs be wires, black wires grow on her head.
I have seen roses damask'd, red and white,
But no such roses see I in her cheeks;
And in some perfumes is there more delight
Than in the breath that from my mistress reeks.
I love to hear her speak, — yet well I know
That music hath a far more pleasing sound;
I grant I never saw a goddess go, —
My mistress when she walks, treads on the ground;
   And yet, by heaven, I think my love as rare
   As any she belied with false compare.

BARNABE BARNES (1569?–1609)

PROLIFIC WRITER of verse including two sonnet-sequences, *Parthenophil and Parthenophe* (1593) and *A Divine Century of Spiritual Sonnets* (1595).

"Ah, sweet Content, where is thy mild abode?"

Ah, sweet Content, where is thy mild abode?
Is it with shepherds and light-hearted swains,
Which sing upon the downs and pipe abroad,
Tending their flocks and cattle on the plains?
Ah, sweet Content, where dost thou safely rest?
In heaven, with angels which the praises sing
Of him that made and rules at his behest
The minds and hearts of every living thing?
Ah, sweet Content, where doth thine harbour hold?
Is it in churches, with religious men
Which please the gods with prayers manifold,
And in their studies meditate it then? —
   Whether thou dost in heaven or earth appear,
   Be where thou wilt, thou wilt not harbour here.

JOHN DONNE *(1573–1631)*

CONSIDERED BY many to be the greatest of the Metaphysical poets. Raised a Catholic, Donne took Anglican orders in 1615, becoming Dean of St. Paul's in 1621. The following poems are from his *Holy Sonnets*.

"Thou hast made me, and shall thy work decay?"

Thou hast made me, and shall thy work decay?
Repair me now, for now mine end doth haste,
I run to death, and death meets me as fast,
And all my pleasures are like yesterday;
I dare not move my dim eyes any way,
Despair behind, and death before doth cast
Such terror, and my feeble flesh doth waste
By sin in it, which it t'wards hell doth weigh;
Only thou art above, and when towards thee
By thy leave I can look, I rise again;
But our old subtle foe so tempteth me,
That not one hour my self I can sustain;
    Thy Grace may wing me to prevent his art,
    And thou like Adamant draw mine iron heart.

"At the round earth's imagin'd corners, blow"

At the round earth's imagin'd corners, blow
Your trumpets, Angels, and arise, arise
From death, you numberless infinities
Of souls, and to your scattered bodies go,
All whom the flood did, and fire shall o'erthrow,
All whom war, dearth, age, agues, tyrannies,
Despair, law, chance, hath slain, and you whose eyes,
Shall behold God, and never taste death's woe.
But let them sleep, Lord, and me mourn a space,
For, if above all these, my sins abound,
'Tis late to ask abundance of thy grace,
When we are there; here on this lowly ground,
    Teach me how to repent; for that's as good
    As if thou hadst seal'd my pardon, with thy blood.

"Death be not proud, though some have called thee"

Death be not proud, though some have called thee
Mighty and dreadful, for, thou art not so,
For those whom thou think'st thou dost overthrow,
Die not, poor death, nor yet canst thou kill me.
From rest and sleep, which but thy pictures be,
Much pleasure, then from thee, much more must flow,
And soonest our best men with thee do go,
Rest of their bones, and soul's delivery.
Thou art slave to Fate, Chance, kings, and desperate men,
And dost with poison, war, and sickness dwell,
And poppy, or charms can make us sleep as well,
And better than thy stroke; why swell'st thou then?
  One short sleep past, we wake eternally,
  And death shall be no more; death, thou shalt die.

"Batter my heart, three-person'd God; for you"

Batter my heart, three-person'd God; for you
As yet but knock, breathe, shine, and seek to mend;
That I may rise, and stand, o'erthrow me and bend
Your force, to break, blow, burn and make me new.
I, like an usurpt town, to another due,
Labour to admit you, but Oh, to no end,
Reason your viceroy in me, me should defend,
But is captiv'd, and proves weak or untrue.
Yet dearly I love you, and would be loved fain,
But am betroth'd unto your enemy:
Divorce me, untie, or break that knot again,
Take me to you, imprison me, for I
  Except you enthrall me, never shall be free,
  Nor ever chaste, except you ravish me.

WILLIAM DRUMMOND OF HAWTHORNDEN
(1585–1649)

SCOTTISH POET and historian. The tragic death of his fiancée on the eve of their wedding inspired many of his sonnets.

"I know that all beneath the moon decays"

I know that all beneath the moon decays,
And what by mortals in this world is brought,
In Time's great periods shall return to nought;
That fairest states have fatal nights and days;
I know how all the Muse's heavenly lays,
With toil of spright which are so dearly bought,
As idle sounds, of few or none are sought,
And that nought lighter is than airy praise;
I know frail beauty like the purple flower,
To which one morn both birth and death affords;
That love a jarring is of mind's accords,
Where sense and will invassal reason's power:
   Know what I list, this all can not me move,
   But that, O me! I both must write and love.

"My lute, be as thou wert when thou didst grow"

My lute, be as thou wert when thou didst grow
With thy green mother in some shady grove,
When immelodious winds but made thee move,
And birds their ramage[1] did on thee bestow.
Since that dear Voice which did thy sounds approve,
Which wont in such harmonious strains to flow,
Is reft from Earth to tune those spheres above,
What art thou but a harbinger of woe?
Thy pleasing notes be pleasing notes no more,
But orphans' wailings to the fainting ear;
Each stroke a sigh, each sound draws forth a tear;
For which be silent as in woods before:
   Or if that any hand to touch thee deign,
   Like widow'd turtle still her loss complain.

---

[1] [Songs.]

GEORGE HERBERT *(1593–1633)*

ORDAINED IN the Anglican church in 1630, Herbert wrote religious verse, none of which was published until after his death.

Prayer

Prayer, the Church's banquet, Angels' age,
God's breath in man returning to his birth,
The soul in paraphrase, heart in pilgrimage,
The Christian plummet sounding heav'n and earth;
Engine against th' Almighty, sinner's tower,
Reversed thunder, Christ-side-piercing spear,
The six-days'-world transposing in an hour,
A kind of tune, which all things hear and fear;
Softness, and peace, and joy, and love, and bliss,
Exalted manna, gladness of the best,
Heaven in ordinary, man well dressed,
The milky way, the bird of Paradise,
    Church bells beyond the stars heard, the soul's blood,
    The land of spices, something understood.

Redemption

Having been tenant long to a rich Lord,
Not thriving, I resolved to be bold,
And make a suit unto Him, to afford
A new small-rented lease, and cancel th' old.
In heaven at His manor I Him sought:
They told me there, that He was lately gone
About some land, which He had dearly bought
Long since on Earth, to take possession.
I straight returned, and knowing His great birth,
Sought Him accordingly in great resorts —
In cities, theatres, gardens, parks, and courts:
At length I heard a ragged noise and mirth
    Of thieves and murderers; there I Him espied,
    Who straight, "Your suit is granted," said, and died.

JOHN MILTON *(1608–1674)*

AUTHOR OF *Paradise Lost*, Milton wrote relatively few sonnets, but they are considered among the finest in English.

On His Being Arrived to the Age of Twenty-Three

How soon hath Time, the subtle thief of youth,
    Stolen on his wing my three and twentieth year!
    My hasting days fly on with full career,
    But my late spring no bud or blossom shew'th.
Perhaps my semblance might deceive the truth,
    That I to manhood am arrived so near,
    And inward ripeness doth much less appear,
    That some more timely-happy spirits indu'th.[1]
Yet be it less or more, or soon or slow,
    It shall be still in strictest measure even
    To that same lot, however mean or high,
Toward which Time leads me, and the will of Heaven.
    All is, if I have grace to use it so,
    As ever in my great Task-master's eye.

On His Blindness

When I consider how my light is spent
    Ere half my days in this dark world and wide,
    And that one Talent which is death to hide
    Lodged with me useless, though my soul more bent
To serve therewith my Maker, and present
    My true account, lest He returning chide,
    "Doth God exact day-labour, light denied?"
    I fondly ask. But Patience, to prevent
That murmur, soon replies, "God doth not need
    Either man's work or his own gifts. Who best
    Bear his mild yoke, they serve him best. His state
Is kingly: thousands at his bidding speed,
    And post o'er land and ocean without rest;
    They also serve who only stand and wait."

---

[1] [Endows.]

On the Late Massacre in Piedmont

Avenge, O Lord, thy slaughtered Saints, whose bones
   Lie scattered on the Alpine mountains cold;
   Even them who kept thy truth so pure of old,
When all our fathers worshiped stocks and stones,
Forget not: in thy book record their groans
   Who were thy sheep, and in their ancient fold
   Slain by the bloody Piemontese, that rolled
Mother with infant down the rocks. Their moans
The vales redoubled to the hills, and they
   To heaven. Their martyred blood and ashes sow
O'er all the Italian fields, where still doth sway
   The triple Tyrant;[1] that from these may grow
A hundredfold, who, having learnt thy way,
   Early may fly the Babylonian woe.

On His Deceased Wife

Methought I saw my late espousèd saint
   Brought to me like Alcestis from the grave,
   Whom Jove's great son to her glad husband gave,
   Rescued from Death by force, though pale and faint.[2]
Mine, as whom washed from spot of childbed taint
   Purification in the Old Law did save,
   And such as yet once more I trust to have
   Full sight of her in Heaven without restraint,
Came vested all in white, pure as her mind.
   Her face was veiled; yet to my fancied sight
   Love, sweetness, goodness, in her person shined
So clear as in no face with more delight.
   But, oh! as to embrace me she inclined,
   I waked, she fled, and day brought back my night.

---

[1] [The Pope.]

[2] [Herakles (Hercules) brought Alcestis back from the dead to her husband Admetus.]

To the Lord General Cromwell, on the Proposals of Certain Ministers at the Committee for the Propagation of the Gospel

Cromwell, our chief of men, who through a cloud
   Not of war only, but detractions rude,
   Guided by faith and matchless fortitude,
   To peace and truth thy glorious way hast ploughed,
And on the neck of crownèd Fortune proud
   Hast reared God's trophies, and his work pursued,
   While Darwen stream, with blood of Scots imbrued,
   And Dunbar field, resounds thy praises loud,
And Worcester's laureate wreath: yet much remains
   To conquer still; Peace hath her victories
   No less renowned than War: new foes arise,
Threatening to bind our souls with secular chains.
   Help us to save free conscience from the paw
   Of hireling wolves, whose Gospel is their maw.

THOMAS GRAY *(1716–1771)*

AUTHOR OF the famous "Elegy Written in a Country Churchyard." The following is Gray's only sonnet.

On the Death of Mr. Richard West

In vain to me the smiling mornings shine,
And reddening Phœbus lifts his golden fire;
The birds in vain their amorous descant join;
Or cheerful fields resume their green attire:
These ears, alas! for other notes repine,
A different object do these eyes require;
My lonely anguish melts no heart but mine,
And in my breast the imperfect joys expire.
Yet morning smiles the busy race to cheer,
And newborn pleasure brings to happier men;
The fields to all their wonted tribute bear;
To warm their little loves the birds complain;
I fruitless mourn to him that cannot hear,
And weep the more because I weep in vain.

WILLIAM BLAKE *(1757–1827)*

POET AND artist. "To the Evening Star" is an unrhymed sonnet with innovative and interesting metrical features.

To the Evening Star

Thou fair-hair'd angel of the evening,
Now, whilst the sun rests on the mountains, light
Thy bright torch of love; thy radiant crown
Put on, and smile upon our evening bed!
Smile on our loves, and while thou drawest the
Blue curtains of the sky, scatter thy silver dew
On every flower that shuts its sweet eyes
In timely sleep. Let thy west wind sleep on
The lake; speak silence with thy glimmering eyes,
And wash the dusk with silver. Soon, full soon,
Dost thou withdraw; then the wolf rages wide,
And the lion glares thro' the dun forest:
The fleeces of our flocks are cover'd with
Thy sacred dew: protect them with thine influence.

ROBERT BURNS *(1759–1796)*

SCOTLAND'S GREATEST poet, author of such perennial favorites as "To a Mouse" and "The Cotter's Saturday Night."

A Sonnet upon Sonnets

Fourteen, a sonneteer thy praises sings;
What magic myst'ries in that number lie!
Your hen hath fourteen eggs beneath her wings
That fourteen chickens to the roost may fly.
Fourteen full pounds the jockey's stone must be;
His age fourteen—a horse's prime is past.
Fourteen long hours too oft the Bard must fast;
Fourteen bright bumpers—bliss he ne'er must see!
Before fourteen, a dozen yields the strife;
Before fourteen—e'en thirteen's strength is vain.
Fourteen good years—a woman gives us life;
Fourteen good men—we lose that life again.
What lucubrations can be more upon it?
Fourteen good measur'd verses make a sonnet.

WILLIAM LISLE BOWLES (1762–1850)

POET AND cleric, Bowles is chiefly remembered for his *Fourteen Sonnets* (1789).

"O Time! who know'st a lenient hand to lay"

O Time! who know'st a lenient hand to lay
Softest on sorrow's wound, and slowly thence,
Lulling to sad repose the weary sense,
The faint pang stealest unperceived away;
On thee I rest my only hope at last,
And think, when thou hast dried the bitter tear
That flows in vain o'er all my soul held dear,
I may look back on every sorrow past,
And meet life's peaceful evening with a smile; —
As some lone bird, at day's departing hour,
Sings in the sunbeam, of the transient shower
Forgetful, though its wings are wet the while: —
   Yet ah! how much must that poor heart endure,
   Which hopes from thee, and thee alone, a cure!

WILLIAM WORDSWORTH (1770–1850)

GREAT ROMANTIC poet, Wordsworth was a master, and a champion, of the sonnet form.
He wrote over 500 sonnets.

"Nuns fret not at their convent's narrow room"

Nuns fret not at their convent's narrow room;
And hermits are contented with their cells;
And students with their pensive citadels;
Maids at the wheel, the weaver at his loom,
Sit blithe and happy; bees that soar for bloom,
High as the highest Peak of Furness-fells,
Will murmur by the hour in foxglove bells:
In truth the prison, into which we doom
Ourselves, no prison is: and hence for me,
In sundry moods, 't was pastime to be bound
Within the Sonnet's scanty plot of ground;
Pleased if some Souls (for such there needs must be)
Who have felt the weight of too much liberty,
Should find brief solace there, as I have found.

Scorn Not the Sonnet

Scorn not the Sonnet; Critic, you have frowned,
Mindless of its just honours; with this key
Shakspeare unlocked his heart; the melody
Of this small lute gave ease to Petrarch's wound;
A thousand times this pipe did Tasso sound;
With it Camöens soothed an exile's grief;
The Sonnet glittered a gay myrtle leaf
Amid the cypress with which Dante crowned
His visionary brow: a glow-worm lamp,
It cheered mild Spenser, called from Faery-land
To struggle through dark ways; and, when a damp
Fell round the path of Milton, in his hand
The Thing became a trumpet; whence he blew
Soul-animating strains — alas, too few!

"It is a beauteous evening, calm and free"

It is a beauteous evening, calm and free,
The holy time is quiet as a Nun
Breathless with adoration; the broad sun
Is sinking down in its tranquillity;
The gentleness of heaven broods o'er the Sea:
Listen! the mighty Being is awake,
And doth with his eternal motion make
A sound like thunder — everlastingly.
Dear Child! dear Girl! that walkest with me here,
If thou appear untouched by solemn thought,
Thy nature is not therefore less divine:
Thou liest in Abraham's bosom all the year;
And worship'st at the Temple's inner shrine,
God being with thee when we know it not.

"Surprised by joy—impatient as the wind"

Surprised by joy—impatient as the wind
I turned to share the transport—O! with whom
But Thee, deep buried in the silent tomb,
That spot which no vicissitude can find?
Love, faithful love, recalled thee to my mind—
But how could I forget thee? Through what power,
Even for the least division of an hour,
Have I been so beguiled as to be blind
To my most grievous loss?—That thought's return
Was the worst pang that sorrow ever bore,
Save one, one only, when I stood forlorn,
Knowing my heart's best treasure was no more;
That neither present time, nor years unborn
Could to my sight that heavenly face restore.

Composed upon Westminster Bridge, Sept. 3, 1802

Earth has not anything to show more fair:
Dull would he be of soul who could pass by
A sight so touching in its majesty:
This City now doth, like a garment, wear
The beauty of the morning; silent, bare,
Ships, towers, domes, theatres, and temples lie
Open unto the fields, and to the sky;
All bright and glittering in the smokeless air.
Never did sun more beautifully steep
In his first splendour, valley, rock, or hill;
Ne'er saw I, never felt, a calm so deep!
The river glideth at his own sweet will:
Dear God! the very houses seem asleep;
And all that mighty heart is lying still!

"The world is too much with us; late and soon"

The world is too much with us; late and soon,
Getting and spending, we lay waste our powers:
Little we see in Nature that is ours;
We have given our hearts away, a sordid boon!
The Sea that bares her bosom to the moon;
The winds that will be howling at all hours,
And are up-gathered now like sleeping flowers;
For this, for everything, we are out of tune;
It moves us not. — Great God! I'd rather be
A Pagan suckled in a creed outworn;
So might I, standing on this pleasant lea,
Have glimpses that would make me less forlorn;
Have sight of Proteus rising from the sea;
Or hear old Triton blow his wreathèd horn.

SAMUEL TAYLOR COLERIDGE (1772–1834)

FRIEND OF Wordsworth, author of "The Rime of the Ancient Mariner" and "Kubla Khan."

Work without Hope

All Nature seems at work. Slugs leave their lair —
The bees are stirring — birds are on the wing —
And Winter slumbering in the open air,
Wears on his smiling face a dream of Spring!
And I the while, the sole unbusy thing,
Nor honey make, nor pair, nor build, nor sing.

Yet well I ken the banks where amaranths blow,
Have traced the fount whence streams of nectar flow.
Bloom, O ye amaranths! bloom for whom ye may,
For me ye bloom not! Glide, rich streams, away!
With lips unbrightened, wreathless brow, I stroll:
And would you learn the spells that drowse my soul?
Work without Hope draws nectar in a sieve,
And Hope without an object cannot live.

On a Discovery Made Too Late

Thou bleedest, my poor Heart! and thy distress
Reasoning I ponder with a scornful smile
And probe thy sore wound sternly, though the while
Swoln be mine eye and dim with heaviness.
Why didst thou listen to Hope's whisper bland?
Or, listening, why forget the healing tale,
When Jealousy with feverous fancies pale
Jarr'd thy fine fibres with a maniac's hand?
Faint was that Hope, and rayless! — Yet 'twas fair
And sooth'd with many a dream the hour of rest:
Thou should'st have lov'd it most, when most opprest,
And nurs'd it with an agony of care,
Even as a mother her sweet infant heir
That wan and sickly droops upon her breast!

ROBERT SOUTHEY (1774–1843)

PROLIFIC ENGLISH poet, appointed poet laureate in 1813. Among his best-known poems
is "The Battle of Blenheim."

Winter

A wrinkled, crabbèd man they picture thee,
Old Winter, with a rugged beard as grey
As the long moss upon the apple-tree;
Blue-lipt, an icedrop at thy sharp blue nose,
Close muffled up, and on thy dreary way
Plodding alone through sleet and drifting snows.
They should have drawn thee by the high-heapt hearth,
Old Winter! seated in thy great armed chair,
Watching the children at their Christmas mirth;
Or circled by them as thy lips declare
Some merry jest, or tale of murder dire,
Or troubled spirit that disturbs the night,
Pausing at times to rouse the mouldering fire,
Or taste the old October[1] brown and bright.

---

[1] [i.e. October ale.]

CHARLES LAMB *(1775–1834)*

ENGLISH POET and essayist, friend of Coleridge and Wordsworth.

"A timid grace sits trembling in her eye"

A timid grace sits trembling in her eye,
As loth to meet the rudeness of men's sight,
Yet shedding a delicious lunar light
That steeps in kind oblivious ecstasy
The care-crazed mind, like some still melody:
Speaking most plain the thoughts which do possess
Her gentle sprite: peace, and meek quietness,
And innocent loves, and maiden purity:
A look whereof might heal the cruel smart
Of changed friends, or fortune's wrongs unkind:
Might to sweet deeds of mercy move the heart
Of him who hates his brethren of mankind.
Turned are those lights from me, who fondly yet
Past joys, vain loves, and buried hopes regret.

JOSEPH BLANCO WHITE *(1775–1841)*

SPANISH-BORN clergyman and theological writer. His "To Night," extravagantly praised
by Coleridge, was one of the most popular sonnets of its time.

To Night

Mysterious Night! when our first parent knew
Thee from report divine, and heard thy name,
Did he not tremble for this lovely frame,
This glorious canopy of light and blue?
Yet 'neath a curtain of translucent dew,
Bathed in the rays of the great setting flame,
Hesperus with the host of heaven came,
And lo! Creation widened in man's view.
Who could have thought such darkness lay concealed
Within thy beams, O Sun! or who could find,
Whilst fly and leaf and insect stood revealed,
That to such countless orbs thou mad'st us blind!
Why do we then shun Death with anxious strife?
If Light can thus deceive, wherefore not Life?

LEIGH HUNT *(1784–1859)*

POET, CRITIC and journalist, friend and associate of Keats, Shelley, Byron and other leading Romantic poets.

The Nile

It flows through old hushed Egypt and its sands,
Like some grave mighty thought threading a dream,
And times and things, as in that vision, seem
Keeping along it their eternal stands, —
Caves, pillars, pyramids, the shepherd bands
That roamed through the young world, the glory extreme
Of high Sesostris, and that southern beam,
The laughing queen that caught the world's great hands.
Then comes a mightier silence, stern and strong,
As of a world left empty of its throng,
And the void weighs on us; and then we wake,
And hear the fruitful stream lapsing along
'Twixt villages, and think how we shall take
Our own calm journey on for human sake.

To the Grasshopper and the Cricket

Green little vaulter in the sunny grass,
Catching your heart up at the feel of June,
Sole voice that's heard amidst the lazy noon,
When even the bees lag at the summoning brass;
And you, warm little housekeeper, who class
With those who think the candles come too soon,
Loving the fire, and with your tricksome tune
Nick the glad silent moments as they pass;
Oh sweet and tiny cousins, that belong
One to the fields, the other to the hearth,
Both have your sunshine; both, though small, are strong
At your clear hearts; and both were sent on earth
To sing in thoughtful ears this natural song:
In-doors and out, summer and winter, — Mirth.

GEORGE GORDON, LORD BYRON *(1788–1824)*

BYRON WAS NOT FOND of the sonnet form and wrote very few sonnets. Chillon, referred to in the following poem, is the site of a castle in which the Swiss patriot François de Bonnivard was imprisoned in the 1530s.

Sonnet on Chillon

Eternal Spirit of the chainless Mind!
   Brightest in dungeons, Liberty, thou art; —
   For there thy habitation is the heart, —
The heart which love of thee alone can bind;
And when thy sons to fetters are consigned,
   To fetters, and the damp vault's dayless gloom,
   Their country conquers with their martyrdom,
And Freedom's fame finds wings on every wind.

Chillon! thy prison is a holy place,
   And thy sad floor an altar, for 'twas trod,
Until his very steps have left a trace,
   Worn, as if thy cold pavement were a sod,
By Bonnivard! May none those marks efface!
   For they appeal from tyranny to God.

PERCY BYSSHE SHELLEY *(1792–1822)*

GREAT ROMANTIC poet who drowned at the age of 29. His sonnet "Ozymandias" is one of the best-known poems in English.

Ozymandias

I met a traveller from an antique land
Who said: Two vast and trunkless legs of stone
Stand in the desert . . . Near them, on the sand,
Half sunk, a shattered visage lies, whose frown,
And wrinkled lip, and sneer of cold command,
Tell that its sculptor well those passions read
Which yet survive, stamped on these lifeless things,
The hand that mocked them, and the heart that fed:
And on the pedestal these words appear:
"My name is Ozymandias, king of kings:
Look on my works, ye Mighty, and despair!"
Nothing beside remains. Round the decay
Of that colossal wreck, boundless and bare
The lone and level sands stretch far away.

Sonnet: England in 1819

An old, mad, blind, despised, and dying king, —
Princes, the dregs of their dull race, who flow
Through public scorn, — mud from a muddy spring, —
Rulers who neither see, nor feel, nor know,
But leech-like to their fainting country cling,
Till they drop, blind in blood, without a blow, —
A people starved and stabbed in the untilled field, —
An army, which liberticide and prey
Makes as a two-edged sword to all who wield, —
Golden and sanguine laws which tempt and slay;
Religion Christless, Godless — a book sealed;
A Senate, — Time's worst statute unrepealed, —
Are graves, from which a glorious Phantom may
Burst, to illumine our tempestuous day.

"Lift not the painted veil which those who live"

Lift not the painted veil which those who live
Call Life: though unreal shapes be pictured there,
And it but mimic all we would believe
With colours idly spread, — behind, lurk Fear
And Hope, twin Destinies; who ever weave
Their shadows, o'er the chasm, sightless and drear.
I knew one who had lifted it — he sought,
For his lost heart was tender, things to love,
But found them not, alas! nor was there aught
The world contains, the which he could approve.
Through the unheeding many he did move,
A splendour among shadows, a bright blot
Upon this gloomy scene, a Spirit that strove
For truth, and like the Preacher found it not.

WILLIAM CULLEN BRYANT *(1794–1878)*

AMERICAN POET and journalist. His best-known poems are "Thanatopsis" and "To a Waterfowl."

Midsummer

A power is on the earth and in the air
　　From which the vital spirit shrinks afraid,
　　And shelters him, in nooks of deepest shade,
From the hot steam and from the fiery glare.
Look forth upon the earth — her thousand plants
　　Are smitten; even the dark sun-loving maize
　　Faints in the field beneath the torrid blaze;
The herd beside the shaded fountain pants;
For life is driven from all the landscape brown;
　　The bird has sought his tree, the snake his den,
　　The trout floats dead in the hot stream, and men
Drop by the sun-stroke in the populous town;
　　As if the Day of Fire had dawned, and sent
　　Its deadly·breath into the firmament.

November

Yet one smile more, departing, distant sun!
　　One mellow smile through the soft vapory air,
Ere, o'er the frozen earth, the loud winds run,
　　Or snows are sifted o'er the meadows bare.
One smile on the brown hills and naked trees,
　　And the dark rocks whose summer wreaths are cast,
And the blue gentian-flower, that, in the breeze,
　　Nods lonely, of her beauteous race the last.
Yet a few sunny days, in which the bee
　　Shall murmur by the hedge that skirts the way,
The cricket chirp upon the russet lea,
　　And man delight to linger in thy ray.
Yet one rich smile, and we will try to bear
The piercing winter frost, and winds, and darkened air.

JOHN KEATS *(1795–1821)*

ONE OF the greatest of English Romantic poets and the author of several great sonnets. Keats died of tuberculosis at the age of 25.

On First Looking into Chapman's Homer

Much have I travell'd in the realms of gold,
   And many goodly states and kingdoms seen;
   Round many western islands have I been
Which bards in fealty to Apollo hold.
Oft of one wide expanse had I been told
   That deep-brow'd Homer ruled as his demesne;
   Yet did I never breathe its pure serene
Till I heard Chapman speak out loud and bold:
Then felt I like some watcher of the skies
   When a new planet swims into his ken;
Or like stout Cortez when with eagle eyes
   He star'd at the Pacific — and all his men
Look'd at each other with a wild surmise —
   Silent, upon a peak in Darien.

On Sitting Down to Read *King Lear* Once Again

O golden tongued Romance, with serene lute!
   Fair plumed Syren, Queen of far-away!
   Leave melodizing on this wintry day,
Shut up thine olden pages, and be mute:
Adieu! for, once again, the fierce dispute
   Betwixt damnation and impassion'd clay
   Must I burn through; once more humbly assay
The bitter-sweet of this Shakespearian fruit:
Chief Poet! and ye clouds of Albion,
   Begetters of our deep eternal theme!
When through the old oak Forest I am gone,
   Let me not wander in a barren dream,
But, when I am consumed in the fire,
Give me new Phœnix wings to fly at my desire.

On Seeing the Elgin Marbles

My spirit is too weak — mortality
   Weighs heavily on me like unwilling sleep,
   And each imagin'd pinnacle and steep
Of godlike hardship, tells me I must die
Like a sick Eagle looking at the sky.
   Yet 'tis a gentle luxury to weep
   That I have not the cloudy winds to keep,
Fresh for the opening of the morning's eye.
Such dim-conceived glories of the brain
   Bring round the heart an undescribable feud;
So do these wonders a most dizzy pain,
   That mingles Grecian grandeur with the rude
Wasting of old Time — with a billowy main —
   A sun — a shadow of a magnitude.

"Why did I laugh to-night? No voice will tell"

Why did I laugh to-night? No voice will tell:
   No God, no Demon of severe response,
Deigns to reply from Heaven or from Hell.
   Then to my human heart I turn at once.
Heart! Thou and I are here sad and alone;
   I say, why did I laugh! O mortal pain!
O Darkness! Darkness! ever must I moan,
   To question Heaven and Hell and Heart in vain.
Why did I laugh? I know this Being's lease,
   My fancy to its utmost blisses spreads;
Yet would I on this very midnight cease,
   And the world's gaudy ensigns see in shreds;
Verse, Fame, and Beauty are intense indeed,
But Death intenser — Death is Life's high meed.

When I Have Fears

When I have fears that I may cease to be
   Before my pen has glean'd my teeming brain,
Before high-piled books, in charactery,
   Hold like rich garners the full ripen'd grain;
When I behold, upon the night's starr'd face,
   Huge cloudy symbols of a high romance,
And think that I may never live to trace
   Their shadows, with the magic hand of chance;
And when I feel, fair creature of an hour,
   That I shall never look upon thee more,
Never have relish in the faery power
   Of unreflecting love; — then on the shore
Of the wide world I stand alone, and think
Till love and fame to nothingness do sink.

Bright Star

Bright star, would I were stedfast as thou art —
   Not in lone splendour hung aloft the night
And watching, with eternal lids apart,
   Like nature's patient, sleepless Eremite,
The moving waters at their priestlike task
   Of pure ablution round earth's human shores,
Or gazing on the new soft-fallen mask
   Of snow upon the mountains and the moors —
No — yet still stedfast, still unchangeable,
   Pillow'd upon my fair love's ripening breast,
To feel for ever its soft fall and swell,
   Awake for ever in a sweet unrest,
Still, still to hear her tender-taken breath,
And so live ever — or else swoon to death.

HARTLEY COLERIDGE (1796–1849)

SON OF Samuel Taylor Coleridge. He wrote numerous sonnets, generally considered to be the finest of his poems.

Prayer

There is an awful quiet in the air,
   And the sad earth, with moist imploring eye,
   Looks wide and wakeful at the pondering sky,
Like Patience slow subsiding to Despair.
But see, the blue smoke as a voiceless prayer,
   Sole witness of a secret sacrifice,
   Unfolds its tardy wreaths, and multiplies
Its soft chameleon breathings in the rare
Capacious ether,—so it fades away,
   And nought is seen beneath the pendent blue
The undistinguishable waste of day.
   So have I dreamed!—oh may the dream be true!—
   That praying souls are purged from mortal hue,
And grow as pure as He to whom they pray.

"Long time a child, and still a child, when years"

Long time a child, and still a child, when years
   Had painted manhood on my cheek, was I;
   For yet I lived like one not born to die;
A thriftless prodigal of smiles and tears,
No hope I needed, and I knew no fears.
   But sleep, though sweet, is only sleep; and waking,
   I waked to sleep no more; at once o'ertaking
The vanguard of my age, with all arrears
Of duty on my back. Nor child, nor man,
   Nor youth, nor sage, I find my head is grey,
For I have lost the race I never ran:
   A rathe[1] December blights my lagging May;
And still I am a child, though I be old:
Time is my debtor for my years untold.

---

[1] [Precocious.]

THOMAS HOOD (1799–1845)

POET AND journalist, Hood is best known for his humorous work, but also wrote serious poetry of high quality, such as the two sonnets presented here.

Silence

There is a silence where hath been no sound,
   There is a silence where no sound may be,
   In the cold grave — under the deep deep sea,
Or in wide desert where no life is found,
Which hath been mute, and still must sleep profound;
   No voice is hushed — no life treads silently,
   But clouds and cloudy shadows wander free,
That never spoke, over the idle ground:
But in green ruins, in the desolate walls
   Of antique palaces, where Man hath been,
Though the dun fox, or wild hyæna, calls,
   And owls, that flit continually between,
Shriek to the echo, and the low winds moan,
There the true Silence is, self-conscious and alone.

Death

It is not death, that sometime in a sigh
   This eloquent breath shall take its speechless flight;
That sometime these bright stars, that now reply
   In sunlight to the sun, shall set in night;
   That this warm conscious flesh shall perish quite,
And all life's ruddy springs forget to flow;
   That thoughts shall cease, and the immortal sprite
Be lapped in alien clay and laid below;
It is not death to know this, — but to know
   That pious thoughts, which visit at new graves
In tender pilgrimage, will cease to go
   So duly and so oft, — and when grass waves
Over the past-away, there may be then
No resurrection in the minds of men.

ELIZABETH BARRETT BROWNING *(1806–1861)*

The Sonnets from the Portuguese, written by Mrs. Browning to her husband, the poet Robert Browning, include some of the best-known love poems in English.

"If thou must love me, let it be for nought"

If thou must love me, let it be for nought
Except for love's sake only. Do not say
"I love her for her smile — her look — her way
Of speaking gently, — for a trick of thought
That falls in well with mine, and certes[1] brought
A sense of pleasant ease on such a day" —
For these things in themselves, Belovèd, may
Be changed, or change for thee, — and love, so wrought,
May be unwrought so. Neither love me for
Thine own dear pity's wiping my cheeks dry, —
A creature might forget to weep, who bore
Thy comfort long, and lose thy love thereby!
But love me for love's sake, that evermore
Thou mayst love on, through love's eternity.

"Belovèd, my Belovèd, when I think"

Belovèd, my Belovèd, when I think
That thou wast in the world a year ago,
What time I sat alone here in the snow
And saw no footprint, heard the silence sink
No moment at thy voice, but, link by link,
Went counting all my chains as if that so
They never could fall off at any blow
Struck by thy possible hand, — why, thus I drink
Of life's great cup of wonder! Wonderful,
Never to feel thee thrill the day or night
With personal act or speech, — nor ever cull
Some prescience of thee with the blossoms white
Thou sawest growing! Atheists are as dull,
Who cannot guess God's presence out of sight.

---

[1] [Certainly.]

"If I leave all for thee, wilt thou exchange"

If I leave all for thee, wilt thou exchange
And be all to me? Shall I never miss
Home-talk and blessing and the common kiss
That comes to each in turn, nor count it strange,
When I look up, to drop on a new range
Of walls and floors, another home than this?
Nay, wilt thou fill that place by me which is
Filled by dead eyes too tender to know change?
That's hardest. If to conquer love, has tried,
To conquer grief, tries more, as all things prove;
For grief indeed is love and grief beside.
Alas, I have grieved so I am hard to love.
Yet love me — wilt thou? Open thine heart wide,
And fold within the wet wings of thy dove.

"How do I love thee? Let me count the ways"

How do I love thee? Let me count the ways.
I love thee to the depth and breadth and height
My soul can reach, when feeling out of sight
For the ends of Being and ideal Grace.
I love thee to the level of everyday's
Most quiet need, by sun and candle-light.
I love thee freely, as men strive for Right;
I love thee purely, as they turn from Praise.
I love thee with the passion put to use
In my old griefs, and with my childhood's faith.
I love thee with a love I seemed to lose
With my lost saints, — I love thee with the breath,
Smiles, tears, of all my life! — and, if God choose,
I shall but love thee better after death.

HENRY WADSWORTH LONGFELLOW *(1807–1882)*

THE MOST popular American poet of his time, author of "The Song of Hiawatha," "The Courtship of Miles Standish" and other popular poems.

Mezzo Cammin[1]

Half of my life is gone, and I have let
    The years slip from me and have not fulfilled
    The aspiration of my youth, to build
    Some tower of song with lofty parapet.
Not indolence, nor pleasure, nor the fret
    Of restless passions that would not be stilled,
    But sorrow, and a care that almost killed,
    Kept me from what I may accomplish yet;
Though, half-way up the hill, I see the Past
    Lying beneath me with its sounds and sights, —
    A city in the twilight dim and vast,
With smoking roofs, soft bells, and gleaming lights, —
    And hear above me on the autumnal blast
    The cataract of Death far thundering from the heights.

The Cross of Snow

In the long, sleepless watches of the night
    A gentle face — the face of one long dead —
    Looks at me from the wall, where round its head
    The night-lamp casts a halo of pale light.
Here in this room she died; and soul more white
    Never through martyrdom of fire was led
    To its repose; nor can in books be read
    The legend of a life more benedight.
There is a mountain in the distant West
    That, sun-defying, in its deep ravines
    Displays a cross of snow upon its side.
Such is the cross I wear upon my breast
    These eighteen years, through all the changing scenes
    And seasons, changeless since the day she died.

---

[1] [Halfway (through life); an allusion to the first line of Dante's *Inferno*.]

Milton

I pace the sounding sea-beach and behold
   How the voluminous billows roll and run,
   Upheaving and subsiding, while the sun
   Shines through their sheeted emerald far unrolled,
And the ninth wave, slow gathering fold by fold
   All its loose-flowing garments into one,
   Plunges upon the shore, and floods the dun
   Pale reach of sands, and changes them to gold.
So in majestic cadence rise and fall
   The mighty undulations of thy song,
   O sightless bard, England's Mæonides!
And ever and anon, high over all
   Uplifted, a ninth wave superb and strong,
   Floods all the soul with its melodious seas.

The Poets

O ye dead Poets, who are living still
   Immortal in your verse, though life be fled,
   And ye, O living Poets, who are dead
   Though ye are living, if neglect can kill,
Tell me if in the darkest hours of ill,
   With drops of anguish falling fast and red
   From the sharp crown of thorns upon your head,
   Ye were not glad your errand to fulfil?
Yes; for the gift and ministry of Song
   Have something in them so divinely sweet,
   It can assuage the bitterness of wrong;
Not in the clamor of the crowded street,
   Not in the shouts and plaudits of the throng,
   But in ourselves, are triumph and defeat.

JOHN GREENLEAF WHITTIER *(1807–1892)*

A QUAKER, Whittier was an ardent abolitionist and one of the most prolific and popular American poets of his time.

Forgiveness

My heart was heavy, for its trust had been
    Abused, its kindness answered with foul wrong;
So, turning gloomily from my fellow-men,
    One summer Sabbath day I strolled among
The green mounds of the village burial-place;
    Where, pondering how all human love and hate
    Find one sad level; and how, soon or late,
Wronged and wrongdoer, each with meekened face,
    And cold hands folded over a still heart,
Pass the green threshold of our common grave,
    Whither all footsteps tend, whence none depart,
Awed for myself, and pitying my race,
Our common sorrow, like a mighty wave,
Swept all my pride away, and trembling I forgave!

Godspeed

Outbound, your bark awaits you. Were I one
    Whose prayer availeth much, my wish should be
    Your favoring trade-wind and consenting sea.
By sail or steed was never love outrun,
And, here or there, love follows her in whom
    All graces and sweet charities unite,
    The old Greek beauty set in holier light;
And her for whom New England's byways bloom,
Who walks among us welcome as the Spring,
    Calling up blossoms where her light feet stray.
    God keep you both, make beautiful your way,
Comfort, console, and bless; and safely bring,
Ere yet I make upon a vaster sea
The unreturning voyage, my friends to me.

CHARLES TENNYSON TURNER (1808–1879)

BROTHER OF Alfred, Lord Tennyson, Turner was a clergyman and poet. He wrote nearly 350 sonnets, many of high quality.

The Buoy-Bell

How like the leper, with his own sad cry
Enforcing his own solitude, it tolls!
That lonely bell set in the rushing shoals,
To warn us from the place of jeopardy!
O friend of man! sore-vex'd by ocean's power,
The changing tides wash o'er thee day by day;
Thy trembling mouth is fill'd with bitter spray,
Yet still thou ringest on from hour to hour;
High is thy mission, though thy lot is wild —
To be in danger's realm a guardian sound;
In seamen's dreams a pleasant part to bear,
And earn their blessing as the year goes round,
And strike the key-note of each grateful prayer,
Breath'd in their distant homes by wife or child!

Orion

How oft I've watch'd thee from the garden croft,
In silence, when the busy day was done,
Shining with wondrous brilliancy aloft,
And flickering like a casement 'gainst the sun!
I've seen thee soar from out some snowy cloud,
Which held the frozen breath of land and sea,
Yet broke and sever'd as the wind grew loud —
But earth-bound winds could not dismember thee,
Nor shake thy frame of jewels; I have guess'd
At thy strange shape and function, haply felt
The charm of that old myth about thy belt
And sword; but, most, my spirit was possess'd
By His great Presence, Who is never far
From his light-bearers, whether man or star.

ALFRED, LORD TENNYSON (1809–1892)

ONE OF the greatest Victorian poets, author of *Idylls of the King*, "In Memoriam," and many of the best-loved poems of the era.

"If I were loved, as I desire to be"

If I were loved, as I desire to be,
What is there in the great sphere of the earth,
And range of evil between death and birth,
That I should fear, — if I were loved by thee?
All the inner, all the outer world of pain
Clear Love would pierce and cleave, if thou wert mine,
As I have heard that, somewhere in the main,
Fresh-water springs come up through bitter brine.
'T were joy, not fear, claspt hand-in-hand with thee,
To wait for death — mute — careless of all ills,
Apart upon a mountain, tho' the surge
Of some new deluge from a thousand hills
Flung leagues of roaring foam into the gorge
Below us, as far on as eye could see.

Poets and Their Bibliographies

Old poets foster'd under friendlier skies,
    Old Virgil who would write ten lines, they say,
    At dawn, and lavish all the golden day
To make them wealthier in the readers' eyes;
And you, old popular Horace, you the wise
    Adviser of the nine-years-ponder'd lay,[1]
    And you, that wear a wreath of sweeter bay,
Catullus, whose dead songster[2] never dies;
If, glancing downward on the kindly sphere
    That once had roll'd you round and round the sun,
You see your Art still shrined in human shelves,
You should be jubilant that you flourish'd here
    Before the Love of Letters, overdone,
Had swamped the sacred poets with themselves.

---

[1] [He recommended a nine years' wait between the composition of a poem and its publication.]
[2] [His mistress' sparrow.]

EDGAR ALLAN POE (1809–1849)

POET, short story writer and critic, author of "The Raven" and other notable verse.

To Science

Science! true daughter of Old Time thou art!
    Who alterest all things with thy peering eyes.
Why preyest thou thus upon the poet's heart,
    Vulture, whose wings are dull realities?
How should he love thee? or how deem thee wise,
    Who wouldst not leave him in his wandering
To seek for treasure in the jewelled skies,
    Albeit he soared with an undaunted wing?
Hast thou not dragged Diana from her car?
    And driven the Hamadryad from the wood
To seek a shelter in some happier star?
Hast thou not torn the Naiad from her flood,
The Elfin from the green grass, and from me
The summer dream beneath the tamarind tree?

Silence

There are some qualities — some incorporate things,
    That have a double life, which thus is made
A type of that twin entity which springs
    From matter and light, evinced in solid and shade.
There is a two-fold *Silence* — sea and shore —
    Body and soul. One dwells in lonely places,
    Newly with grass o'ergrown; some solemn graces,
Some human memories and tearful lore,
Render him terrorless: his name's "No More."
He is the corporate Silence: dread him not!
    No power hath he of evil in himself;
But should some urgent fate (untimely lot!)
    Bring thee to meet his shadow (nameless elf,
That haunteth the lone regions where hath trod
No foot of man,) commend thyself to God!

WILLIAM BELL SCOTT *(1811–1890)*

SCOTTISH PAINTER and poet, friend of Dante Gabriel Rossetti and others of the Pre-Raphaelite group.

My Mother

There was a gather'd stillness in the room:
Only the breathing of the great sea rose
From far off, aiding that profound repose,
With regular pulse and pause within the gloom
Of twilight, as if some impending doom
Was now approaching; — I sat moveless there,
Watching with tears and thoughts that were like prayer,
Till the hour struck, — the thread dropp'd from the loom;
And the Bark pass'd in which freed souls are borne.
The dear still'd face lay there; that sound forlorn
Continued; I rose not, but long sat by:
And now my heart oft hears that sad seashore,
When she is in the far-off land, and I
Wait the dark sail returning yet once more.

A Garland for Advancing Years

Wear thou this fresh green garland this one day
  This white-flowered garland wear for Love's delight,
  While still the sun shines, ere the lessening light
Declines into the shadows cold and grey:
Wear thou this myrtle leaf while yet ye may.
  Love's wings are wings that hate the dews of night;
  Nor will he rest still smiling in our sight,
And still companioning our western way.
Wear thou this plain green garland this one day
  To please Love's eyes, else not for all the might
  Of all the gods, nor any law of right
Will he, content with age's disarray,
For us pass by the youthful and the gay;
  And it were hard to live in love's despite.

JONES VERY *(1813–1880)*

AMERICAN POET, preacher and mystic, Very claimed his sonnets were divinely inspired.

The Columbine

Still, still my eye will gaze long fixed on thee,
Till I forget that I am called a man,
And at thy side fast-rooted seem to be,
And the breeze comes my cheek with thine to fan.
Upon this craggy hill our life shall pass,
A life of summer days and summer joys,
Nodding our honey-bells mid pliant grass
In which the bee half hid his time employs;
And here we'll drink with thirsty pores the rain,
And turn dew-sprinkled to the rising sun,
And look when in the flaming west again
His orb across the heaven its path has run;
Here left in darkness on the rocky steep,
My weary eyes shall close like folding flowers in sleep.

The Fair Morning

The clear bright morning, with its scented air
  And gaily waving flowers, is here again;
Man's heart is lifted with the voice of prayer,
  And peace descends, as falls the gentle rain;
The tuneful birds, that all the night have slept,
  Take up at dawn the evening's dying lay,
When sleep upon their eyelids gently crept
  And stole with stealthy craft their song away.
High overhead the forest's swaying boughs
  Sprinkle with drops the traveler on his way;
He hears far off the tinkling bells of cows
  Driven to pasture at the break of day;
With vigorous step he passes swift along,
Making the woods reëcho with his song.

The Clouded Morning

The morning comes, and thickening clouds prevail,
　　Hanging like curtains all the horizon round,
Or overhead in heavy stillness sail;
　　So still is day, it seems like night profound;
Scarce by the city's din the air is stirred,
　　And dull and deadened comes its every sound;
The cock's shrill, piercing voice subdued is heard,
　　By the thick folds of muffling vapors drowned.
Dissolved in mists the hills and trees appear,
　　Their outlines lost and blended with the sky;
And well-known objects, that to all are near,
　　No longer seem familiar to the eye,
But with fantastic forms they mock the sight,
As when we grope amid the gloom of night.

JAMES RUSSELL LOWELL (1819–1891)

AMERICAN CRITIC and poet, author of *The Vision of Sir Launfal* and *A Fable for Critics*.

The Street

They pass me by like shadows, crowds on crowds,
　　Dim ghosts of men, that hover to and fro,
Hugging their bodies round them like thin shrouds,
　　Wherein their souls were buried long ago:
They trampled on their youth, and faith, and love,
　　They cast their hope of human-kind away,
With Heaven's clear messages they madly strove,
　　And conquered, — and their spirits turned to clay:
Lo! how they wander round the world, their grave,
　　Whose ever-gaping maw by such is fed,
Gibbering at living men, and idly rave,
　　"We only truly live, but ye are dead."
Alas! poor fools, the anointed eye may trace
A dead soul's epitaph in every face!

FREDERICK GODDARD TUCKERMAN (1821–1873)

RECLUSIVE AMERICAN poet, Tuckerman has won growing recognition in recent years, particularly for the innovative technique he displays in his sonnets.

"An upper chamber in a darkened house"

An upper chamber in a darkened house,
Where, ere his footsteps reached ripe manhood's brink,
Terror and anguish were his lot to drink;
I cannot rid the thought nor hold it close
But dimly dream upon that man alone:
Now though the autumn clouds most softly pass,
The cricket chides beneath the doorstep stone
And greener than the season grows the grass.
Nor can I drop my lids nor shade my brows,
But there he stands beside the lifted sash;
And with a swooning of the heart, I think
Where the black shingles slope to meet the boughs
And, shattered on the roof like smallest snows,
The tiny petals of the mountain ash.

"Last night I dreamed we parted once again"

Last night I dreamed we parted once again;
That all was over. From the outward shore
I saw a dim bark lessen more and more,
That bore her from me o'er the boundless main,
And yearned to follow: no sense of mystery
Fell on me nor the old fear of the sea.
Only I thought, knowledge must bring relief,
Nor feared the sunless gulfs, the tempest's breath,
Nor drowning, nor the bitterness of death.
Yet while as one who sees his hope decay,
And scarcely weeping, vacant in my grief,
I on the jetty stood and watched the ship,
The wave broke fresher, flinging on my lip
Some drops of salt. I shuddered, and turned away.

MATTHEW ARNOLD (1822–1888)

VICTORIAN POET and essayist, professor of poetry at Oxford (1857–1867) and author of the enormously popular poem "Dover Beach."

Shakespeare

Others abide our question. Thou art free.
We ask and ask: Thou smilest and art still,
Out-topping knowledge. For the loftiest hill
That to the stars uncrowns his majesty,
Planting his stedfast footsteps in the sea,
Making the Heaven of Heavens his dwelling-place,
Spares but the cloudy border of his base
To the foil'd searching of mortality:
And thou, who didst the stars and sunbeams know,
Self-school'd, self-scann'd, self-honour'd, self-secure,
Didst walk on Earth unguess'd at. Better so!
All pains the immortal spirit must endure,
All weakness that impairs, all griefs that bow,
Find their sole voice in that victorious brow.

West London

Crouch'd on the pavement close by Belgrave Square
A tramp I saw, ill, moody, and tongue-tied;
A babe was in her arms, and at her side
A girl; their clothes were rags, their feet were bare.
Some labouring men, whose work lay somewhere there,
Pass'd opposite; she touch'd her girl, who hied
Across, and begg'd, and came back satisfied.
The rich she had let pass with frozen stare.
Thought I: Above her state this spirit towers;
She will not ask of aliens, but of friends,
Of sharers in a common human fate.
She turns from that cold succour, which attends
The unknown little from the unknowing great,
And points us to a better time than ours.

GEORGE MEREDITH (1828–1909)

NOVELIST AND poet. The poems from the sonnet sequence *Modern Love* (last three selections) are sixteen-line variants of the form.

Lucifer in Starlight

On a starred night Prince Lucifer uprose.
Tired of his dark dominion swung the fiend
Above the rolling ball in cloud part screened,
Where sinners hugged their spectre of repose.
Poor prey to his hot fit of pride were those.
And now upon his western wing he leaned,
Now his huge bulk o'er Afric's sands careened,
Now the black planet shadowed Arctic snows.
Soaring through wider zones that pricked his scars
With memory of the old revolt from Awe,
He reached a middle height, and at the stars,
Which are the brain of heaven, he looked, and sank.
Around the ancient track marched, rank on rank,
The army of unalterable law.

"By this he knew she wept with waking eyes"

By this he knew she wept with waking eyes:
That, at his hand's light quiver by her head,
The strange low sobs that shook their common bed
Were called into her with a sharp surprise,
And strangled mute, like little gaping snakes,
Dreadfully venomous to him. She lay
Stone-still, and the long darkness flowed away
With muffled pulses. Then, as midnight makes
Her giant heart of Memory and Tears
Drink the pale drug of silence, and so beat
Sleep's heavy measure, they from head to feet
Were moveless, looking through their dead black years
By vain regret scrawled over the blank wall.
Like sculptured effigies they might be seen
Upon their marriage-tomb, the sword between;
Each wishing for the sword that severs all.

"In our old shipwrecked days there was an hour"

In our old shipwrecked days there was an hour,
When in the firelight steadily aglow,
Joined slackly, we beheld the red chasm grow
Among the clicking coals. Our library-bower
That eve was left to us: and hushed we sat
As lovers to whom Time is whispering.
From sudden-opened doors we heard them sing:
The nodding elders mixed good wine with chat.
Well knew we that Life's greatest treasure lay
With us, and of it was our talk. "Ah, yes!
Love dies!" I said: I never thought it less.
She yearned to me that sentence to unsay.
Then when the fire domed blackening, I found
Her cheek was salt against my kiss, and swift
Up the sharp scale of sobs her breast did lift: —
Now am I haunted by that taste! that sound!

"Thus piteously Love closed what he begat"

Thus piteously Love closed what he begat:
The union of this ever-diverse pair!
These two were rapid falcons in a snare,
Condemned to do the flitting of the bat.
Lovers beneath the singing sky of May,
They wandered once; clear as the dew on flowers:
But they fed not on the advancing hours:
Their hearts held cravings for the buried day.
Then each applied to each that fatal knife,
Deep questioning, which probes to endless dole.
Ah, what a dusty answer gets the soul
When hot for certainties in this our life! —
In tragic hints here see what evermore
Moves dark as yonder midnight ocean's force,
Thundering like ramping hosts of warrior horse,
To throw that faint thin line upon the shore!

DANTE GABRIEL ROSSETTI *(1828–1882)*

PRE-RAPHAELITE PAINTER and poet. His long sonnet-sequence, *The House of Life*, from which the following selections are taken, contains some of the finest sonnets of the period.

A Sonnet

A Sonnet is a moment's monument, —
Memorial from the Soul's eternity
To one dead, deathless hour. Look that it be,
Whether for lustral rite or dire portent,
Of its own arduous fulness reverent:
Carve it in ivory or in ebony,
As Day or Night may rule; and let Time see
Its flowering crest impearl'd and orient.
A Sonnet is a coin: its face reveals
The soul, — its converse, to what power 't is due: —
Whether for tribute to the august appeals
Of Life, or dower in Love's high retinue,
It serve; or, 'mid the dark wharf's cavernous breath,
In Charon's palm it pay the toll to Death.

Silent Noon

Your hands lie open in the long fresh grass, —
 The finger-points look through like rosy blooms:
 Your eyes smile peace. The pasture gleams and glooms
'Neath billowing skies that scatter and amass.
All round our nest, far as the eye can pass,
 Are golden kingcup-fields with silver edge
 Where the cow-parsley skirts the hawthorn-hedge.
'Tis visible silence, still as the hour-glass.
Deep in the sun-searched growths the dragon-fly
Hangs like a blue thread loosened from the sky: —
 So this wing'd hour is dropt to us from above.
Oh! clasp we to our hearts, for deathless dower,
This close-companioned inarticulate hour
 When twofold silence was the song of love.

A Superscription

Look in my face; my name is Might-have-been;
  I am also called No-more, Too-late, Farewell;
  Unto thine ear I hold the dead-sea shell
Cast up thy Life's foam-fretted feet between;
Unto thine eyes the glass where that is seen
  Which had Life's form and Love's, but by my spell
  Is now a shaken shadow intolerable,
Of ultimate things unuttered the frail screen.
Mark me, how still I am! But should there dart
  One moment through thy soul the soft surprise
  Of that winged Peace which lulls the breath of sighs, —
Then shalt thou see me smile, and turn apart
Thy visage to mine ambush at thy heart
  Sleepless with cold commemorative eyes.

The One Hope

When vain desire at last and vain regret
  Go hand in hand to death, and all is vain,
  What shall assuage the unforgotten pain
And teach the unforgetful to forget?
Shall Peace be still a sunk stream long unmet, —
  Or may the soul at once in a green plain
  Stoop through the spray of some sweet life-fountain
And cull the dew-drenched flowering amulet?
Ah! when the wan soul in that golden air
  Between the scriptured petals softly blown
  Peers breathless for the gift of grace unknown, —
Ah! let none other written spell soe'er
But only the one Hope's one name be there, —
  Not less nor more, but even that word alone.

CHRISTINA ROSSETTI *(1830–1894)*

SISTER OF Dante Gabriel Rossetti, a devout Anglican and writer of much religious verse. Her best-known work is "Goblin Market."

Rest

O earth, lie heavily upon her eyes;
　　Seal her sweet eyes weary of watching, Earth;
　　Lie close around her; leave no room for mirth
With its harsh laughter, nor for sound of sighs.
She hath no questions, she hath no replies,
　　Hushed in and curtained with a blessèd dearth
　　Of all that irked her from the hour of birth;
With stillness that is almost Paradise.
Darkness more clear than noonday holdeth her,
　　Silence more musical than any song;
Even her very heart has ceased to stir:
　　　Until the morning of Eternity
　　　Her rest shall not begin nor end, but be;
And when she wakes she will not think it long.

Youth Gone

Youth gone, and beauty gone if ever there
Dwelt beauty in so poor a face as this;
Youth gone and beauty, what remains of bliss?
I will not bind fresh roses in my hair,
To shame a cheek at best but little fair, —
Leave youth his roses, who can bear a thorn, —
I will not seek for blossoms anywhere,
Except such common flowers as blow with corn.
Youth gone and beauty gone, what doth remain?
The longing of a heart pent up forlorn,
A silent heart whose silence loves and longs;
The silence of a heart which sang its songs
While youth and beauty made a summer morn,
Silence of love that cannot sing again.

After Death

The curtains were half drawn, the floor was swept
And strewn with rushes, rosemary and may
Lay thick upon the bed on which I lay,
Where through the lattice ivy-shadows crept.
He lean'd above me, thinking that I slept
And could not hear him; but I heard him say:
"Poor child, poor child:" and as he turn'd away
Came a deep silence, and I knew he wept.
He did not touch the shroud, or raise the fold
That hid my face, or take my hand in his,
Or ruffle the smooth pillows for my head:
He did not love me living; but once dead
He pitied me; and very sweet it is
To know he still is warm though I am cold.

Remember

Remember me when I am gone away,
Gone far away into the silent land;
When you can no more hold me by the hand,
Nor I half turn to go yet turning stay.
Remember me when no more, day by day,
You tell me of our future that you plann'd:
Only remember me; you understand
It will be late to counsel then or pray.
Yet if you should forget me for a while
And afterwards remember, do not grieve:
For if the darkness and corruption leave
A vestige of the thoughts that once I had,
Better by far you should forget and smile
Than that you should remember and be sad.

THEODORE WATTS-DUNTON *(1832–1914)*

POET AND prose writer, associated with the Pre-Raphaelite group. He befriended and cared for Swinburne for many years.

The Sonnet's Voice
(A Metrical Lesson by the Seashore)

Yon silvery billows breaking on the beach
Fall back in foam beneath the star-shine clear,
The while my rhymes are murmuring in your ear
A restless lore like that the billows teach;
For on these sonnet-waves my soul would reach
From its own depths, and rest within you, dear,
As, through the billowy voices yearning here,
Great nature strives to find a human speech.
A sonnet is a wave of melody:
From heaving waters of the impassion'd soul
A billow of tidal music one and whole
Flows in the "octave;" then returning free,
Its ebbing surges in the "sestet" roll
Back to the deeps of Life's tumultuous sea.

Coleridge

I see thee pine like her in golden story
Who, in her prison, woke and saw, one day,
The gates thrown open — saw the sunbeams play,
With only a web 'tween her and summer's glory;
Who, when that web — so frail, so transitory
It broke before her breath — had fallen away,
Saw other webs and others rise for aye
Which kept her prison'd till her hair was hoary.
Those songs half-sung that yet were all-divine —
That woke Romance, the queen, to reign afresh —
Had been but preludes from that lyre of thine,
Could thy rare spirit's wings have pierced the mesh
Spun by the wizard who compels the flesh,
But lets the poet see how heav'n can shine.

WILLIAM MORRIS *(1834–1896)*

POET, ARTIST and craftsman, Morris' achievements in many fields make him a leading figure of the Victorian era, particularly influential in the decorative arts.

Summer Dawn

Pray but one prayer for me 'twixt thy closed lips,
   Think but one thought of me up in the stars.
The summer night waneth, the morning light slips,
   Faint and grey 'twixt the leaves of the aspen, betwixt the
      cloud-bars,
That are patiently waiting there for the dawn:
   Patient and colourless, though Heaven's gold
Waits to float through them along with the sun.
Far out in the meadows, above the young corn,
   The heavy elms wait, and restless and cold
The uneasy wind rises; the roses are dun;
Through the long twilight they pray for the dawn,
Round the lone house in the midst of the corn.
   Speak but one word to me over the corn,
   Over the tender, bow'd locks of the corn.

ALGERNON CHARLES SWINBURNE *(1837–1909)*

POET AND critic, Swinburne was an associate of Dante Gabriel Rossetti and the Pre-Raphaelite group.

Love and Sleep

Lying asleep between the strokes of night
   I saw my love lean over my sad bed,
   Pale as the duskiest lily's leaf or head,
Smooth-skinned and dark, with bare throat made to bite,
Too wan for blushing and too warm for white,
   But perfect-coloured without white or red.
   And her lips opened amorously, and said—
I wist not what, saving one word—Delight.
And all her face was honey to my mouth,
   And all her body pasture to mine eyes;
      The long lithe arms and hotter hands than fire,
The quivering flanks, hair smelling of the south,
   The bright light feet, the splendid supple thighs
      And glittering eyelids of my soul's desire.

JOHN ADDINGTON SYMONDS *(1840–1893)*

ENGLISH POET, critic and translator. Translated the sonnets of Michelangelo and Campanella and wrote original sonnets of high quality.

The Sonnet (III)

The Sonnet is a world, where feelings caught
In webs of phantasy, combine and fuse
Their kindred elements 'neath mystic dews
Shed from the ether round man's dwelling wrought;
Distilling heart's content, star-fragrance fraught
With influences from the breathing fires
Of heaven in everlasting endless gyres
Enfolding and encircling orbs of thought.
Our Sonnet's world hath two fix'd hemispheres:
This, where the sun with fierce strength masculine
Pours his keen rays and bids the noonday shine;
That, where the moon and the stars, concordant powers,
Shed milder rays, and daylight disappears
In low melodious music of still hours.

Lux Est Umbra Dei[1]

Nay, Death, thou art a shadow! Even as light
Is but the shadow of invisible God,
And of that shade the shadow is thin Night,
Veiling the earth whereon our feet have trod;
So art Thou but the shadow of this life,
Itself the pale and unsubstantial shade
Of living God, fulfill'd by love and strife
Throughout the universe Himself hath made:
And as frail Night, following the flight of earth,
Obscures the world we breathe in, for a while,
So Thou, the reflex of our mortal birth,
Veilest the life wherein we weep and smile:
But when both earth and life are whirl'd away,
What shade can shroud us from God's deathless day?

---

[1] [*Light is the shadow of God.*]

WILFRID SCAWEN BLUNT *(1840–1922)*

ENGLISH POET, diplomat and political writer. The poems here are from his 1880 sonnet sequence, *The Love Sonnets of Proteus*.

On Her Vanity

What are these things thou lovest? Vanity.
To see men turn their heads when thou dost pass;
To be the signboard and the looking glass
Where every idler there may glut his eye;
To hear men speak thy name mysteriously,
Wagging their heads. Is it for this, alas,
That thou hast made a placard of a face
On which the tears of love were hardly dry?
What are these things thou lovest? The applause
Of prostitutes at wit which is not thine;
The sympathy of shop-boys who would weep
Their shilling's worth of woe in any cause,
At any tragedy. — Their tears and mine,
What difference? Oh truly tears are cheap!

As To His Choice of Her

If I had chosen thee, thou shouldst have been
A virgin proud, untamed, immaculate,
Chaste as the morning star, a saint, a queen,
Scarred by no wars, no violence of hate.
Thou shouldst have been of soul commensurate
With thy fair body, brave and virtuous
And kind and just; and, if of poor estate,
At least an honest woman for my house.
I would have had thee come of honoured blood
And honourable nurture. Thou shouldst bear
Sons to my pride and daughters to my heart,
And men should hold thee happy, wise, and good.
Lo, thou art none of this, but only fair,
Yet must I love thee, dear, and as thou art.

To One Who Would Make a Confession

Oh! leave the Past to bury its own dead.
The Past is naught to us, the Present all.
What need of last year's leaves to strew Love's bed?
What need of ghosts to grace a festival?
I would not, if I could, those days recall,
Those days not ours. For us the feast is spread,
The lamps are lit, and music plays withal.
Then let us love and leave the rest unsaid.
This island is our home. Around it roar
Great gulfs and oceans, channels, straits, and seas.
What matter in what wreck we reached the shore,
So we both reached it? We can mock at these.
Oh! leave the Past, if Past indeed there be.
I would not know it. I would know but thee.

THOMAS HARDY (1840–1928)

GREAT ENGLISH novelist and poet, author of *The Return of the Native*, *Tess of the D'Urbervilles* and other works.

Hap

If but some vengeful god would call to me
From up the sky, and laugh: "Thou suffering thing,
Know that thy sorrow is my ecstasy,
That thy love's loss is my hate's profiting!"

Then would I bear it, clench myself, and die,
Steeled by the sense of ire unmerited;
Half-eased in that a Powerfuller than I
Had willed and meted me the tears I shed.

But not so. How arrives it joy lies slain,
And why unblooms the best hope ever sown?
—Crass Casualty obstructs the sun and rain,
And dicing Time for gladness casts a moan. . . .
These purblind Doomsters had as readily strown
Blisses about my pilgrimage as pain.

Often When Warring

Often when warring for he wist not what,
An enemy-soldier, passing by one weak,
Has tendered water, wiped the burning cheek,
And cooled the lips so black and clammed and hot;

Then gone his way, and maybe quite forgot
The deed of grace amid the roar and reek;
Yet larger vision than loud arms bespeak
He there has reached, although he has known it not.

For natural mindsight, triumphing in the act
Over the throes of artificial rage,
Has thuswise muffled victory's peal of pride,
Rended to ribands policy's specious page
That deals but with evasion, code, and pact,
And war's apology wholly stultified.

MATHILDE BLIND *(1841–1896)*

GERMAN-BORN English poet, translator and biographer. She is remembered chiefly for her sonnets.

The Dead

The dead abide with us! Though stark and cold
  Earth seems to grip them, they are with us still:
  They have forged our chains of being for good or ill,
And their invisible hands these hands yet hold.
Our perishable bodies are the mould
  In which their strong imperishable will —
  Mortality's deep yearning to fulfil —
Hath grown incorporate through dim time untold.
Vibrations infinite of life in death,
  As a star's travelling light survives its star!
  So may we hold our lives, that when we are
The fate of those who then will draw this breath,
  They shall not drag us to their judgment bar,
And curse the heritage which we bequeath.

EDWARD DOWDEN *(1843–1913)*

IRISH POET and scholar, Dowden is best remembered for his studies of Shakespeare.

Leonardo's "Mona Lisa"

Make thyself known, Sibyl, or let despair
Of knowing thee be absolute: I wait
Hour-long and waste a soul. What word of fate
Hides 'twixt the lips which smile and still forbear?
Secret perfection! Mystery too fair!
Tangle the sense no more, lest I should hate
The delicate tyranny, the inviolate
Poise of thy folded hands, the fallen hair.
Nay, nay,—I wrong thee with rough words; still be
Serene, victorious, inaccessible;
Still smile but speak not; lightest irony
Lurk ever 'neath thy eyelids' shadow; still
O'ertop our knowledge; Sphinx of Italy,
Allure us and reject us at thy will!

Two Infinities

A lonely way, and as I went my eyes
Could not unfasten from the Spring's sweet things,
Lush-sprouted grass, and all that climbs and clings
In loose, deep hedges, where the primrose lies
In her own fairness, buried blooms surprise
The plunderer bee and stop his murmurings,
And the glad flutter of a finch's wings
Outstartle small blue-speckled butterflies.
Blissfully did one speedwell plot beguile
My whole heart long; I lov'd each separate flower,
Kneeling. I look'd up suddenly—Dear God!
There stretch'd the shining plain for many a mile,
The mountains rose with what invincible power!
And how the sky was fathomless and broad!

ROBERT BRIDGES *(1844–1930)*

ENGLISH POET, appointed Poet Laureate in 1913. It was Bridges who first collected and
published the poems of Gerard Manley Hopkins.

"While yet we wait for spring, and from the dry"

While yet we wait for spring, and from the dry
And blackening east that so embitters March,
Well-housed must watch grey fields and meadows parch,
And driven dust and withering snowflake fly;
Already in glimpses of the tarnish'd sky
The sun is warm and beckons to the larch,
And where the covert hazels interarch
Their tassell'd twigs, fair beds of primrose lie.
   Beneath the crisp and wintry carpet hid
A million buds but stay their blossoming;
And trustful birds have built their nests amid
The shuddering boughs, and only wait to sing
Till one soft shower from the south shall bid,
And hither tempt the pilgrim steps of spring.

"In autumn moonlight, when the white air wan"

In autumn moonlight, when the white air wan
Is fragrant in the wake of summer hence,
'Tis sweet to sit entranced, and muse thereon
In melancholy and godlike indolence:
   When the proud spirit, lull'd by mortal prime
To fond pretence of immortality,
Vieweth all moments from the birth of time,
All things whate'er have been or yet shall be.
   And like the garden, where the year is spent,
The ruin of old life is full of yearning,
Mingling poetic rapture of lament
With flowers and sunshine of spring's sure returning;
   Only in visions of the white air wan
By godlike fancy seized and dwelt upon.

GERARD MANLEY HOPKINS *(1844–1889)*

A JESUIT PRIEST, Hopkins is much admired today for the intensity of emotion and the innovative techniques evident in his sonnets. None of his poetry was published in his lifetime, the first edition appearing in 1918.

God's Grandeur

The world is charged with the grandeur of God.
  It will flame out, like shining from shook foil;
  It gathers to a greatness, like the ooze of oil
Crushed. Why do men then now not reck his rod?
Generations have trod, have trod, have trod;
  And all is seared with trade; bleared, smeared with toil;
  And wears man's smudge and shares man's smell: the soil
Is bare now, nor can foot feel, being shod.

And for all this, nature is never spent;
  There lives the dearest freshness deep down things;
And though the last lights off the black West went
  Oh, morning, at the brown brink eastward, springs —
Because the Holy Ghost over the bent
  World broods with warm breast and with ah! bright wings.

Spring

Nothing is so beautiful as spring —
  When weeds, in wheels, shoot long and lovely and lush;
  Thrush's eggs look little low heavens, and thrush
Through the echoing timber does so rinse and wring
The ear, it strikes like lightnings to hear him sing;
  The glassy peartree leaves and blooms, they brush
  The descending blue; that blue is all in a rush
With richness; the racing lambs too have fair their fling.

What is all this juice and all this joy?
  A strain of the earth's sweet being in the beginning
In Eden garden. — Have, get, before it cloy,
  Before it cloud, Christ, lord, and sour with sinning,
Innocent mind and Mayday in girl and boy,
  Most, O maid's child, thy choice and worthy the winning.

[Carrion Comfort]

Not, I'll not, carrion comfort, Despair, not feast on thee;
Not untwist — slack they may be — these last strands of man
In me ór, most weary, cry *I can no more*. I can;
Can something, hope, wish day come, not choose not to be.
But ah, but O thou terrible, why wouldst thou rude on me
Thy wring-world right foot rock? lay a lionlimb against me? scan
With darksome devouring eyes my bruisèd bones? and fan,
O in turns of tempest, me heaped there; me frantic to avoid thee
          and flee?

  Why? That my chaff might fly; my grain lie, sheer and clear.
Nay in all that toil, that coil, since (seems) I kissed the rod,
Hand rather, my heart lo! lapped strength, stole joy, would
          laugh, chéer.
Cheer whom though? the hero whose heaven-handling flung
          me, fóot tród
Me? or me that fought him? O which one? is it each one? That
          night, that year
Of now done darkness I wretch lay wrestling with (my God!) my
          God.

"No worst, there is none. Pitched past pitch of grief"

No worst, there is none. Pitched past pitch of grief,
More pangs will, schooled at forepangs, wilder wring.
Comforter, where, where is your comforting?
Mary, mother of us, where is your relief?

My cries heave, herds-long; huddle in a main, a chief
Woe, world-sorrow; on an age-old anvil wince and sing —
Then lull, then leave off. Fury had shrieked "No ling-
ering! Let me be fell: force I must be brief."

  O the mind, mind has mountains; cliffs of fall
Frightful, sheer, no-man-fathomed. Hold them cheap
May who ne'er hung there. Nor does long our small
Durance deal with that steep or deep. Here! creep,
Wretch, under a comfort serves in a whirlwind: all
Life death does end and each day dies with sleep.

EUGENE LEE-HAMILTON (1845–1907)

ENGLISH POET, author of two books of sonnets, *Imaginary Sonnets* (1888) and *Sonnets of the Wingless Hours* (1894).

What the Sonnet Is

Fourteen small broidered berries on the hem
Of Circe's mantle, each of magic gold;
Fourteen of lone Calypso's tears that rolled
Into the sea, for pearls to come of them;
Fourteen clear signs of omen in the gem
With which Medea human fate foretold;
Fourteen small drops, which Faustus, growing old,
Craved of the Fiend, to water Life's dry stem.
It is the pure white diamond Dante brought
To Beatrice; the sapphire Laura wore
When Petrarch cut it sparkling out of thought;
The ruby Shakespeare hewed from his heart's core;
The dark, deep emerald that Rossetti wrought
For his own soul, to wear for evermore.

Sunken Gold

In dim green depths rot ingot-laden ships;
And gold doubloons, that from the drowned hand fell,
Lie nestled in the ocean-flower's bell
With love's old gifts, once kissed by long-drowned lips;
And round some wrought gold cup the sea-grass whips,
And hides lost pearls, near pearls still in their shell,
Where sea-weed forests fill each ocean dell
And seek dim sunlight with their restless tips.
So lie the wasted gifts, the long-lost hopes
Beneath the now hushed surface of myself,
In lonelier depths than where the diver gropes;
They lie deep, deep; but I at times behold
In doubtful glimpses, on some reefy shelf,
The gleam of irrecoverable gold.

ALICE MEYNELL (1847–1922)

ENGLISH POET and essayist. With her husband, the poet Wilfred Meynell, she championed the work of George Meredith, Francis Thompson and others.

Renouncement

I must not think of thee; and, tired yet strong,
I shun the thought that lurks in all delight—
The thought of thee—and in the blue Heaven's height,
And in the sweetest passage of a song.
Oh, just beyond the fairest thoughts that throng
This breast, the thought of thee waits, hidden yet bright;
But it must never, never come in sight;
I must stop short of thee the whole day long.
But when sleep comes to close each difficult day,
When night gives pause to the long watch I keep,
And all my bonds I needs must loose apart,
Must doff my will as raiment laid away,—
With the first dream that comes with the first sleep
I run, I run, I am gathered to thy heart.

Changeless

A poet of one mood in all my lays,
Ranging all life to sing one only love,
Like a west wind across the world I move,
Sweeping my harp of floods mine own wild ways.
The countries change, but not the westwind days
Which are my songs. My soft skies shine above,
And on all seas the colors of a dove,
And on all fields a flash of silver grays.
I make the whole world answer to my art
And sweet monotonous meanings. In your ears
I change not ever, bearing, for my part,
One thought that is the treasure of my years,
A small cloud full of rain upon my heart
And in mine arms, clasped, like a child in tears.

EMMA LAZARUS *(1849–1887)*

AMERICAN POET, essayist and philanthropist. Lazarus was an avid advocate of Jewish causes. Her famous sonnet is inscribed on the pedestal of the Statue of Liberty.

The New Colossus

Not like the brazen giant of Greek fame,
With conquering limbs astride from land to land;
Here at our sea-washed, sunset gates shall stand
A mighty woman with a torch, whose flame
Is the imprisoned lightning, and her name
Mother of Exiles. From her beacon-hand
Glows world-wide welcome; her mild eyes command
The air-bridged harbor that twin cities frame.
"Keep, ancient lands, your storied pomp!" cries she
With silent lips. "Give me your tired, your poor,
Your huddled masses yearning to breathe free,
The wretched refuse of your teeming shore.
Send these, the homeless, tempest-tost to me,
I lift my lamp beside the golden door!"

Echoes

Late-born and woman-souled I dare not hope,
The freshness of the elder lays, the might
Of manly, modern passion shall alight
Upon my Muse's lips, nor may I cope
(Who veiled and screened by womanhood must grope)
With the world's strong-armed warriors and recite
The dangers, wounds, and triumphs of the fight;
Twanging the full-stringed lyre through all its scope.
But if thou ever in some lake-floored cave
O'erbrowed by rocks, a wild voice wooed and heard,
Answering at once from heaven and earth and wave,
Lending elf-music to thy harshest word,
Misprize thou not these echoes that belong
To one in love with solitude and song.

JAMES WHITCOMB RILEY (1849–1916)

"THE HOOSIER Poet," particularly popular for the poems in the dialect of his home state, Indiana.

Silence

    Thousands and thousands of hushed years ago,
        Out on the edge of Chaos, all alone
        I stood on peaks of vapor, high upthrown
    Above a sea that knew nor ebb nor flow,
    Nor any motion won of winds that blow,
        Nor any sound of watery wail or moan,
        Nor lisp of wave, nor wandering undertone
    Of any tide lost in the night below.
    So still it was, I mind me, as I laid
        My thirsty ear against mine own faint sigh
    To drink of that, I sipped it, half afraid
        'Twas but the ghost of a dead voice spilled by
    The one starved star that tottered through the shade
        And came tiptoeing toward me down the sky.

Eternity

    O what a weary while it is to stand,
        Telling the countless ages o'er and o'er,
        Till all the finger-tips held out before
    Our dazzled eyes by heaven's starry hand
    Drop one by one, yet at some dread command
        Are held again, and counted evermore!
        How feverish the music seems to pour
    Along the throbbing veins of anthems grand!
        And how the cherubim sing on and on —
    The seraphim and angels — still in white —
        Still harping — still enraptured — far withdrawn
    In hovering armies tranced in endless flight!
        . . . God's mercy! is there never dusk or dawn,
        Or any crumb of gloom to feed upon?

PHILIP BOURKE MARSTON (1850–1887)

ENGLISH POET, blind from early childhood. His verse was much praised by Dante Gabriel Rossetti.

Love's Music

Love held a harp between his hands, and, lo!
The master hand, upon the harp-strings laid
By way of prelude, such a sweet tune play'd
As made the heart with happy tears o'erflow;
Then sad and wild did that strange music grow,
And, — like the wail of woods by storm gusts sway'd,
While yet the awful thunder's wrath is stay'd,
And earth lies faint beneath the coming blow, —
Still wilder wax'd the tune; until at length
The strong strings, strain'd by sudden stress and sharp
Of that musician's hand intolerable,
And jarr'd by sweep of unrelenting strength,
Sunder'd, and all the broken music fell.
Such was Love's music, — lo, the shatter'd harp!

A Vain Wish

I would not, could I, make thy life as mine;
Only I would, if such a thing might be,
Thou shouldst not, love, forget me utterly;
Yea, when the sultry stars of summer shine
On dreaming woods, where nightingales repine,
I would that at such times should come to thee
Some thought not quite unmix'd with pain, of me, —
Some little sorrow for a soul's decline.
Yea, too, I would that through thy brightest times,
Like the sweet burden of remember'd rhymes,
That gentle sadness should be with thee, dear;
And when the gates of sleep are on thee shut,
I would not, even then, it should be mute,
But murmur, shell-like, at thy spirit's ear.

OSCAR WILDE *(1856–1900)*

IRISH DRAMATIST, poet and writer, author of *The Importance of Being Earnest, The Picture of Dorian Gray* and other works.

Hélas[1]

To drift with every passion till my soul
Is a stringed lute on which all winds can play,
Is it for this that I have given away
Mine ancient wisdom, and austere control?
Methinks my life is a twice-written scroll
Scrawled over on some boyish holiday
With idle songs for pipe and virelay,
Which do but mar the secret of the whole.
Surely there was a time I might have trod
The sunlit heights, and from life's dissonance
Struck one clear chord to reach the ears of God:
Is that time dead? lo! with a little rod
I did but touch the honey of romance —
And must I lose a soul's inheritance?

E Tenebris[2]

Come down, O Christ, and help me! reach thy hand,
   For I am drowning in a stormier sea
   Than Simon on thy lake of Galilee:
The wine of life is spilt upon the sand,
My heart is as some famine-murdered land
   Whence all good things have perished utterly,
   And well I know my soul in Hell must lie
If I this night before God's throne should stand.
"He sleeps perchance, or rideth to the chase,
   Like Baal, when his prophets howled that name
   From morn to noon on Carmel's smitten height."
Nay, peace, I shall behold, before the night,
   The feet of brass, the robe more white than flame,
The wounded hands, the weary human face.

---

[1] [*Alas.*]
[2] [*Out of darkness.*]

CHARLES G. D. ROBERTS *(1860–1943)*

PREEMINENT CANADIAN poet and writer. Much of his poetry deals with nature and pastoral themes.

Burnt Lands

On other fields and other scenes the morn
Laughs from her blue, — but not such scenes are these,
Where comes no cheer of Summer leaves and bees,
And no shade mitigates the day's white scorn.
These serious acres vast no groves adorn;
But giant trunks, bleak shapes that once were trees,
Tower naked, unassuaged of rain or breeze,
Their stern gray isolation grimly borne.
The months roll over them, and mark no change;
But when spring stirs, or autumn stills, the year,
Perchance some phantom leafage rustles faint
Through their parched dreams, — some old-time notes ring
    strange,
When in his slender treble, far and clear,
Reiterates the rain-bird his complaint.

The Night Sky

O Deep of Heaven, 'tis thou alone art boundless,
'Tis thou alone our balance shall not weigh
'Tis thou alone our fathom-line finds soundless, —
Whose infinite our finite must obey!
Through thy blue realms and down thy starry reaches
Thought voyages forth beyond thy furthest fire,
And homing from no sighted shoreline, teaches
Thee measureless as is the soul's desire.
O deep of Heaven! No beam of Pleiad ranging
Eternity may bridge thy gulf of spheres!
The ceaseless hum that fills thy sleep unchanging
Is rain of the innumerable years.
Our worlds, our suns, our ages, — these but stream
Through thine abiding like a dateless dream.

WILLIAM BUTLER YEATS *(1865–1939)*

IRISH POET and dramatist, winner of the Nobel Prize (1923). "Leda and the Swan" is considered among the greatest of modern sonnets.

Leda and the Swan

A sudden blow: the great wings beating still
Above the staggering girl, her thighs caressed
By the dark webs, her nape caught in his bill,
He holds her helpless breast upon his breast.

How can those terrified vague fingers push
The feathered glory from her loosening thighs?
And how can body, laid in that white rush,
But feel the strange heart beating where it lies?

A shudder in the loins engenders there
The broken wall, the burning roof and tower
And Agamemnon dead.

                    Being so caught up,
So mastered by the brute blood of the air,
Did she put on his knowledge with his power
Before the indifferent beak could let her drop?

Meru

Civilisation is hooped together, brought
Under a rule, under the semblance of peace
By manifold illusion; but man's life is thought,
And he, despite his terror, cannot cease
Ravening through century after century,
Ravening, raging, and uprooting that he may come
Into the desolation of reality:
Egypt and Greece, good-bye, and good-bye, Rome!
Hermits upon Mount Meru or Everest,
Caverned in night under the drifted snow,
Or where that snow and winter's dreadful blast
Beat down upon their naked bodies, know
That day brings round the night, that before dawn
His glory and his monuments are gone.

ERNEST DOWSON *(1867–1900)*

ENGLISH POET and translator. In his brief, dissolute life, he produced a slender quantity of poetry, but much of it of high quality.

To One in Bedlam

With delicate, mad hands, behind his sordid bars,
Surely he hath his posies, which they tear and twine;
Those scentless wisps of straw, that miserably line
His strait, caged universe, whereat the dull world stares,

Pedant and pitiful. O, how his rapt gaze wars
With their stupidity! Know they what dreams divine
Lift his long, laughing reveries like enchaunted wine,
And make his melancholy germane to the stars'?

O lamentable brother! if those pity thee,
Am I not fain of all thy lone eyes promise me;
Half a fool's kingdom, far from men who sow and reap,
All their days, vanity? Better than mortal flowers,
Thy moon-kissed roses seem: better than love or sleep,
The star-crowned solitude of thine oblivious hours!

A Last Word

Let us go hence: the night is now at hand;
    The day is overworn, the birds all flown;
    And we have reaped the crops the gods have sown,
Despair and death; deep darkness o'er the land,
Broods like an owl; we cannot understand
    Laughter or tears, for we have only known
    Surpassing vanity: vain things alone
Have driven our perverse and aimless band.

Let us go hence, somewhither strange and cold,
    To Hollow Lands where just men and unjust
    Find end of labour, where's rest for the old,
Freedom to all from love and fear and lust.
Twine our torn hands! O pray the earth enfold
Our life-sick hearts and turn them into dust.

EDWIN ARLINGTON ROBINSON (1869–1935)

AMERICAN POET, three-time winner of the Pulitzer Prize.

Reuben Bright

Because he was a butcher and thereby
Did earn an honest living (and did right),
I would not have you think that Reuben Bright
Was any more a brute than you or I;
For when they told him that his wife must die,
He stared at them, and shook with grief and fright,
And cried like a great baby half that night,
And made the women cry to see him cry.

And after she was dead, and he had paid
The singers and the sexton and the rest,
He packed a lot of things that she had made
Most mournfully away in an old chest
Of hers, and put some chopped-up cedar boughs
In with them, and tore down the slaughter-house.

How Annandale Went Out

"They called it Annandale — and I was there
To flourish, to find words, and to attend:
Liar, physician, hypocrite, and friend,
I watched him; and the sight was not so fair
As one or two that I have seen elsewhere:
An apparatus not for me to mend —
A wreck, with hell between him and the end,
Remained of Annandale; and I was there.

"I knew the ruin as I knew the man;
So put the two together, if you can,
Remembering the worst you know of me.
Now view yourself as I was, on the spot —
With a slight kind of engine. Do you see?
Like this . . . You wouldn't hang me? I thought not."

LORD ALFRED DOUGLAS *(1870–1945)*

ENGLISH POET and friend of Oscar Wilde. His association with Wilde resulted in Wilde's conviction and imprisonment for homosexual practices in 1895.

The Dead Poet

I dreamed of him last night, I saw his face
All radiant and unshadowed of distress,
And as of old, in music measureless,
I heard his golden voice and marked him trace
Under the common thing the hidden grace,
And conjure wonder out of emptiness,
Till mean things put on beauty like a dress
And all the world was an enchanted place.

And then methought outside a fast locked gate
I mourned the loss of unrecorded words,
Forgotten tales and mysteries half said,
Wonders that might have been articulate,
And voiceless thoughts like murdered singing birds.
And so I woke and knew that he was dead.

To Sleep

Ah, Sleep, to me thou com'st not in the guise
Of one who brings good gifts to weary men,
Balm for bruised hearts and fancies alien
To unkind truth, and drying for sad eyes.
I dread the summons to that fierce assize
Of all my foes and woes, that waits me when
Thou mak'st my soul the unwilling denizen
Of thy dim troubled house where unrest lies.

My soul is sick with dreaming, let it rest.
False Sleep, thou hast conspired with Wakefulness,
I will not praise thee, I too long beguiled
With idle tales. Where is thy soothing breast?
Thy peace, thy poppies, thy forgetfulness?
Where is thy lap for me so tired a child?

PAUL LAURENCE DUNBAR *(1872–1906)*

AFRICAN-AMERICAN POET and novelist, popular for his use of dialect and humor, but a writer of serious verse as well. His volume *Complete Poems* was published in 1913.

Douglass[1]

    Ah, Douglass, we have fall'n on evil days,
        Such days as thou, not even thou didst know,
        When thee, the eyes of that harsh long ago
    Saw, salient, at the cross of devious ways,
    And all the country heard thee with amaze.
        Not ended then, the passionate ebb and flow,
        The awful tide that battled to and fro;
    We ride amid a tempest of dispraise.

    Now, when the waves of swift dissension swarm,
        And Honor, the strong pilot, lieth stark,
    Oh, for thy voice high-sounding o'er the storm,
        For thy strong arm to guide the shivering bark,
    The blast-defying power of thy form,
        To give us comfort through the lonely dark.

Slow Through the Dark

    Slow moves the pageant of a climbing race;
        Their footsteps drag far, far below the height,
        And, unprevailing by their utmost might,
    Seem faltering downward from each hard won place.
    No strange, swift-sprung exception we; we trace
        A devious way thro' dim, uncertain light, —
        Our hope, through the long vistaed years, a sight
    Of that our Captain's soul sees face to face.
        Who, faithless, faltering that the road is steep,
    Now raiseth up his drear insistent cry?
        Who stoppeth here to spend a while in sleep
    Or curseth that the storm obscures the sky?
        Heed not the darkness round you, dull and deep;
    The clouds grow thickest when the summit's nigh.

---

[1] [Frederick Douglass, African-American abolitionist and writer.]

ROBERT FROST *(1875–1963)*

ONE OF the most popular modern American poets, Frost displays great versatility in his use of the sonnet form, particularly in regard to the rhyme schemes.

Once by the Pacific

The shattered water made a misty din.
Great waves looked over others coming in,
And thought of doing something to the shore
That water never did to land before.
The clouds were low and hairy in the skies,
Like locks blown forward in the gleam of eyes.
You could not tell, and yet it looked as if
The shore was lucky in being backed by cliff,
The cliff in being backed by continent;
It looked as if a night of dark intent
Was coming, and not only a night, an age.
Someone had better be prepared for rage.
There would be more than ocean-water broken
Before God's last *Put out the Light* was spoken.

Acquainted with the Night

I have been one acquainted with the night.
I have walked out in rain — and back in rain.
I have outwalked the furthest city light.

I have looked down the saddest city lane.
I have passed by the watchman on his beat
And dropped my eyes, unwilling to explain.

I have stood still and stopped the sound of feet
When far away an interrupted cry
Came over houses from another street,

But not to call me back or say good-by;
And further still at an unearthly height
One luminary clock against the sky

Proclaimed the time was neither wrong nor right.
I have been one acquainted with the night.

The Oven Bird

There is a singer everyone has heard,
Loud, a mid-summer and a mid-wood bird,
Who makes the solid tree trunks sound again.
He says that leaves are old and that for flowers
Mid-summer is to spring as one to ten.
He says the early petal-fall is past
When pear and cherry bloom went down in showers
On sunny days a moment overcast;
And comes that other fall we name the fall.
He says the highway dust is over all.
The bird would cease and be as other birds
But that he knows in singing not to sing.
The question that he frames in all but words
Is what to make of a diminished thing.

Acceptance

When the spent sun throws up its rays on cloud
And goes down burning into the gulf below,
No voice in nature is heard to cry aloud
At what has happened. Birds, at least, must know
It is the change to darkness in the sky.
Murmuring something quiet in her breast,
One bird begins to close a faded eye;
Or overtaken too far from his nest,
Hurrying low above the grove, some waif
Swoops just in time to his remembered tree.
At most he thinks or twitters softly, "Safe!
Now let the night be dark for all of me.
Let the night be too dark for me to see
Into the future. Let what will be, be."

SIEGFRIED SASSOON (1886–1967)

ENGLISH POET, known mainly for his antiwar and satirical verses.

Dreamers

Soldiers are citizens of death's gray land,
    Drawing no dividend from time's tomorrows.
In the great hour of destiny they stand,
    Each with his feuds, and jealousies, and sorrows.
Soldiers are sworn to action; they must win
    Some flaming, fatal climax with their lives.
Soldiers are dreamers; when the guns begin
    They think of firelit homes, clean beds, and wives.

I see them in foul dugouts, gnawed by rats,
    And in the ruined trenches, lashed with rain,
Dreaming of things they did with balls and bats,
    And mocked by hopeless longing to regain
Bank holidays, and picture shows, and spats,
    And going to the office in the train.

RUPERT BROOKE (1887–1915)

ENGLISH POET, famous for his war sonnets. He died of blood poisoning while in service
with the Royal Naval Division.

The Soldier

If I should die, think only this of me:
    That there's some corner of a foreign field
That is for ever England. There shall be
    In that rich earth a richer dust concealed;
A dust whom England bore, shaped, made aware,
    Gave, once, her flowers to love, her ways to roam,
A body of England's, breathing English air,
    Washed by the rivers, blest by suns of home.

And think, this heart, all evil shed away,
    A pulse in the eternal mind, no less
        Gives somewhere back the thoughts by England given;
Her sights and sounds; dreams happy as her day;
    And laughter, learnt of friends; and gentleness,
        In hearts at peace, under an English heaven.

EDNA ST. VINCENT MILLAY (1892–1950)

ONE OF the most popular modern American poets, Millay wrote what many consider to be among the finest sonnets of this century.

"Oh, sleep forever in the Latmian cave"

Oh, sleep forever in the Latmian cave,
Mortal Endymion, darling of the Moon!
Her silver garments by the senseless wave
Shouldered and dropped and on the shingle strewn,
Her fluttering hand against her forehead pressed,
Her scattered looks that trouble all the sky,
Her rapid footsteps running down the west —
Of all her altered state, oblivious lie!
Whom earthen you, by deathless lips adored,
Wild-eyed and stammering to the grasses thrust,
And deep into her crystal body poured
The hot and sorrowful sweetness of the dust:
Whereof she wanders mad, being all unfit
For mortal love, that might not die of it.

"Love is not all: it is not meat nor drink"

Love is not all: it is not meat nor drink
Nor slumber nor a roof against the rain;
Nor yet a floating spar to men that sink
And rise and sink and rise and sink again;
Love can not fill the thickened lung with breath,
Nor clean the blood, nor set the fractured bone;
Yet many a man is making friends with death
Even as I speak, for lack of love alone.
It well may be that in a difficult hour,
Pinned down by pain and moaning for release,
Or nagged by want past resolution's power,
I might be driven to sell your love for peace,
Or trade the memory of this night for food.
It well may be. I do not think I would.

"What lips my lips have kissed, and where, and why"

What lips my lips have kissed, and where, and why,
I have forgotten, and what arms have lain
Under my head till morning; but the rain
Is full of ghosts tonight, that tap and sigh
Upon the glass and listen for reply,
And in my heart there stirs a quiet pain
For unremembered lads that not again
Will turn to me at midnight with a cry.
Thus in the winter stands the lonely tree,
Nor knows what birds have vanished one by one,
Yet knows its boughs more silent than before:
I cannot say what loves have come and gone,
I only know that summer sang in me
A little while, that in me sings no more.

"Euclid alone has looked on Beauty bare"

Euclid alone has looked on Beauty bare.
Let all who prate of Beauty hold their peace,
And lay them prone upon the earth and cease
To ponder on themselves, the while they stare
At nothing, intricately drawn nowhere
In shapes of shifting lineage; let geese
Gabble and hiss, but heroes seek release
From dusty bondage into luminous air.
O blinding hour, O holy, terrible day,
When first the shaft into his vision shone
Of light anatomized! Euclid alone
Has looked on Beauty bare. Fortunate they
Who, though once only and then but far away,
Have heard her massive sandal set on stone.

ARCHIBALD MACLEISH (1892–1982)

AMERICAN POET and dramatist. MacLeish held important government posts (he served as Assistant Secretary of State, 1944–1945) and taught at Harvard.

The End of the World

Quite unexpectedly as Vasserot
The armless ambidextrian was lighting
A match between his great and second toe
And Ralph the lion was engaged in biting
The neck of Madame Sossman while the drum
Pointed, and Teeny was about to cough
In waltz-time swinging Jocko by the thumb —
Quite unexpectedly the top blew off:

And there, there overhead, there, there, hung over
Those thousands of white faces, those dazed eyes,
There in the starless dark the poise, the hover,
There with vast wings across the canceled skies,
There in the sudden blackness the black pall
Of nothing, nothing, nothing — nothing at all.

WILFRED OWEN (1893–1918)

ENGLISH POET, killed in action during the First World War, a week before the armistice. His friend Siegfried Sassoon collected and published his poems in 1920.

Anthem for Doomed Youth

What passing-bells for these who die as cattle?
    Only the monstrous anger of the guns.
    Only the stuttering rifles' rapid rattle
Can patter out their hasty orisons.
No mockeries now for them; no prayers nor bells,
    Nor any voice of mourning save the choirs, —
The shrill, demented choirs of wailing shells;
    And bugles calling for them from sad shires.

What candles may be held to speed them all?
    Not in the hands of boys, but in their eyes
Shall shine the holy glimmers of good-byes.
    The pallor of girls' brows shall be their pall;
Their flowers the tenderness of patient minds,
And each slow dusk a drawing-down of blinds.

On Seeing a Piece of Our Artillery Brought into Action

Be slowly lifted up, thou long black arm,
Great gun towering towards Heaven, about to curse;
Sway steep against them, and for years rehearse
Huge imprecations like a blasting charm!
Reach at that Arrogance which needs thy harm,
And beat it down before its sins grow worse;
Spend our resentment, cannon, — yea, disburse
Our gold in shapes of flame, our breaths in storm.

Yet, for men's sakes whom thy vast malison
Must wither innocent of enmity,
Be not withdrawn, dark arm, thy spoilure done,
Safe to the bosom of our prosperity.
But when thy spell be cast complete and whole,
May God curse thee, and cut thee from our soul!

Alphabetical List of Titles and First Lines

(Titles are given, in italics, only when distinct from the first lines.)

A lonely way, and as I went my eyes	65
A poet of one mood in all my lays	70
A power is on the earth and in the air	34
A Sonnet is a moment's monument	55
A sudden blow: the great wings beating still	76
A timid grace sits trembling in her eye	30
A wrinkled, crabbèd man they picture thee	29
Acceptance	82
Acquainted with the Night	81
After Death	58
Ah, Douglass, we have fall'n on evil days	80
Ah, Sleep, to me thou com'st not in the guise	79
Ah, sweet Content, where is thy mild abode?	16
All nature seems at work. Slugs leave their lair	28
An old, mad, blind, despised, and dying King	33
An upper chamber in a darkened house	51
Anthem for Doomed Youth	86
As to His Choice of Her	62
At the round earth's imagin'd corners, blow	17
Avenge, O Lord, thy slaughtered Saints, whose bones	22
Batter my heart, three-person'd God; for you	18
Be slowly lifted up, thou long black arm	87
Because he was a butcher and thereby	78
Belovèd, my Belovèd, when I think	40
Bright Star	37
Bright star, would I were stedfast as thou art	37
Buoy-Bell, The	45
Burnt Lands	75
By this he knew she wept with waking eyes	53
Care-charmer Sleep, son of the sable Night	9
[*Carrion Comfort*]	68
Changeless	70

Civilisation is hooped together, brought   76
Clouded Morning, The   50
Coleridge   59
Columbine, The   49
Come down, O Christ, and help me! reach thy hand   74
Come, Sleep, O Sleep! the certain knot of peace   8
Composed Upon Westminster Bridge, Sept. 3, 1802   27
Cromwell, our chief of men, who through a cloud   23
Cross of Snow, The   42
Crouch'd on the pavement close by Belgrave Square   52

Dead, The   64
Dead Poet, The   79
Dear, why should you command me to my rest   11
Death   39
Death be not proud, though some have called thee   18
Douglass   80
Dreamers   83

E Tenebris   74
Echoes   71
Earth has not anything to show more fair   27
End of the World, The   86
Eternal Spirit of the chainless Mind!   32
Eternity   72
Euclid alone has looked on Beauty bare   85

Fair is my Love and cruel as she's fair   9
Fair is my love, when her fair golden hairs   6
Fair Morning, The   49
Farewell, love, and all thy laws forever   2
Forgiveness   44
Fourteen, a sonneteer thy praises sings   24
Fourteen small broidered berries on the hem   69

Garland for Advancing Years, A   48
God's Grandeur   67
Godspeed   44
Green little vaulter in the sunny grass   31

Half of my life is gone, and I have let   42
Hap   63
Happy ye leaves! whenas those lily hands   5
Having been tenant long to a rich Lord   20
Hélas   74

How Annandale Went Out   78
How do I love thee? Let me count the ways   41
How like the leper, with his own sad cry   45
How oft I've watch'd thee from the garden croft   45
How soon hath Time, the subtle thief of youth   21

I dreamed of him last night, I saw his face   79
I have been one acquainted with the night   81
I know that all beneath the moon decays   19
I met a traveller from an antique land   32
I must not think of thee; and, tired yet strong   70
I pace the sounding sea-beach and behold   43
I see thee pine like her in golden story   59
I would not, could I, make thy life as mine   73
If but some vengeful god would call to me   63
If I had chosen thee, thou shouldst have been   62
If I leave all for thee, wilt thou exchange   41
If I should die, think only this of me   83
If I were loved, as I desire to be   46
If this be love, to draw a weary breath   10
If thou must love me, let it be for nought   40
In autumn moonlight, when the white air wan   66
In dim green depths rot ingot-laden ships   69
In our old shipwrecked days there was an hour   54
In the long, sleepless watches of the night   42
In vain to me the smiling mornings shine   23
It flows through old hushed Egypt and its sands   31
It is a beauteous evening, calm and free   26
It is not death, that sometime in a sigh   39

Last night I dreamed we parted once again   51
Last Word, A   77
Late-born and woman-souled I dare not hope   71
Leave Me, O Love, which reachest but to dust   8
Leda and the Swan   76
Leonardo's "Mona Lisa"   65
Let me not to the marriage of true minds   15
Let others sing of Knights and Paladines   10
Let us go hence: the night is now at hand   77
Lift not the painted veil which those who live   33
Long time a child, and still a child, when years   38
Look in my face; my name is Might-have-been   56
Love and Sleep   60
Love held a harp between his hands, and, lo!   73

Love is not all: it is not meat nor drink 84
Love, that doth reign and live within my thought 3
Loving in truth, and fain in verse my love to show 7
Love's Music 73
Lucifer in Starlight 53
Lux Est Umbra Dei 61
Lying asleep between the strokes of night 60

Make thyself known, Sibyl, or let despair 65
Meru 76
Methought I saw my late espousèd saint 22
Mezzo Cammin 42
Midsummer 34
Milton 43
Most glorious Lord of life, that on this day 5
Much have I travell'd in the realms of gold 35
My galley charged with forgetfulness 1
My heart was heavy, for its trust had been 44
My lute, be as thou wert when thou didst grow 19
My mistress' eyes are nothing like the sun 16
My Mother 48
My spirit is too weak — mortality 36
Mysterious Night! when our first parent knew 30

Nay, Death, thou art a shadow! Even as light 61
New Colossus, The 71
Night Sky, The 75
Nile, The 31
No worst, there is none. Pitched past pitch of grief 68
Not, I'll not, carrion comfort, Despair, not feast on thee 68
Not like the brazen giant of Greek fame 71
Not marble, nor the gilded monuments 14
Nothing is so beautiful as spring 67
November 34
Nuns fret not at their convent's narrow room 25

O Deep of Heaven, 'tis thou alone art boundless 75
O earth, lie heavily upon her eyes 57
O golden tongued Romance, with serene lute 35
O Time! who know'st a lenient hand to lay 25
O what a weary while it is to stand 72
O ye dead Poets, who are living still 43
Often When Warring 64
Often when warring for he wist not what 64

Oh! leave the Past to bury its own dead   63
Oh, sleep forever in the Latmian cave   84
Old poets foster'd under friendlier skies   46
On a Discovery Made Too Late   29
On a starred night Prince Lucifer uprose   53
On First Looking Into Chapman's Homer   35
On Her Vanity   62
On His Being Arrived to the Age of Twenty-Three   21
On His Blindness   21
On His Deceased Wife   22
On other fields and other scenes the morn   75
On Seeing a Piece of Our Artillery Brought into Action   87
On Seeing the Elgin Marbles   36
On Sitting Down to Read King Lear Once Again   35
On the Death of Mr. Richard West   23
On the Late Massacre in Piedmont   22
Once by the Pacific   81
One day I wrote her name upon the strand   6
One Hope, The   56
Orion   45
Others abide our question. Thou art free   52
Outbound, your bark awaits you. Were I one   44
Oven Bird, The   82
Ozymandias   32

Poets, The   43
Poets and Their Bibliographies   46
Pray but one prayer for me 'twixt thy closed lips   60
Prayer (H. Coleridge)   38
Prayer (Herbert)   20
Prayer, the Church's banquet, Angels' age   20

Quite unexpectedly as Vasserot   86

Redemption   20
Remember   58
Remember me when I am gone away   58
Renouncement   70
Rest   57
Reuben Bright   78

Science! True daughter of Old Time thou art!   47
Scorn Not the Sonnet   26
Scorn not the sonnet; Critic, you have frowned   26
Shakespeare   52
Shall I compare thee to a summer's day?   13

Silence (Hood)   39
Silence (Poe)   47
Silence (Riley)   72
Silent Noon   55
Since there's no help, come let us kiss and part   11
[Sir Walter Ralegh to his Son]   4
Slow moves the pageant of a climbing race   80
Slow Through the Dark   80
Soldier, The   83
Soldiers are citizens of death's gray land   83
Sonnet, A   55
Sonnet: England in 1819   33
Sonnet on Chillon   32
Sonnet, The, (III)   61
Sonnet upon Sonnets, A   24
Sonnet's Voice, The   59
Soote Season, The   3
Spring   67
Still, still my eye will gaze long fixed on thee   49
Street, The   50
Summer Dawn   60
Sunken Gold   69
Surprised by joy — impatient as the wind   27
Superscription, A   56

The clear bright morning, with its scented air   49
The curtains were half drawn, the floor was swept   58
The dead abide with us! Though stark and cold   64
Th' expense of spirit in a waste of shame   15
The long love that in my thought doth harbor   1
The morning comes, and thickening clouds prevail   50
The shattered water makes a misty din   81
The Sonnet is a world, where feelings caught   61
The soote season, that bud and bloom forth brings   3
The world is charged with the grandeur of God   67
The world is too much with us; late and soon   28
There are some qualities — some incorporate things   47
There is a singer everyone has heard   82
There is a silence where hath been no sound   39
There is an awful quiet in the air   38
There was a gather'd stillness in the room   48
"They called it Annandale — and I was there"   78
They pass me by like shadows, crowds on crowds   50

Thou bleedest, my poor Heart! and thy distress   29
Thou fair-hair'd angel of the evening   24
Thou hast made me, and shall thy work decay?   17
Thousands and thousands of hushed years ago   72
Three things there be that prosper up apace   4
Thus piteously Love closed what he begat   54
To drift with every passion till my soul   74
To Night   30
To One in Bedlam   77
To One Who Would Make a Confession   63
To Science   47
To Sleep   79
To the Evening Star   24
To the Grasshopper and the Cricket   31
To the Lord General Cromwell. . .   23
Two Infinities   65

Vain Wish, A   73

Wear thou this fresh green garland this one day   48
Were I as base as is the lowly plain   12
West London   52
What are these things thou lovest? Vanity   62
What lips my lips have kissed, and where, and why   85
What passing-bells for these who die as cattle?   86
What the Sonnet Is   69
When I consider how my light is spent   21
When I do count the clock that tells the time   12
When I Have Fears   37
When I have fears that I may cease to be   37
When in disgrace with fortune and men's eyes   13
When the spent sun throws up its rays on cloud   82
When to the sessions of sweet silent thought   14
When vain desire at last and vain regret   56
While yet we wait for spring, and from the dry   66
Whoso list to hunt, I know where is an hind   2
Why did I laugh to-night? No voice will tell   36
Winter   29
With delicate, mad hands, behind his sordid bars   77
With how sad steps, O Moon, thou climb'st the skies!   7
Work without Hope   28

Yet one smile more, departing, distant sun!   34
Yon silvery billows breaking on the beach   59

You must not wonder, though you think it strange   4
Your hands lie open in the long fresh grass   55
Youth Gone   57
Youth gone, and beauty gone if ever there   57

DOVER · THRIFT · EDITIONS

All books complete and unabridged. All 5³⁄₁₆″ × 8¹⁄₄″, paperbound.
Just $1.00–$2.00 in U.S.A.

THE MAN WHO WOULD BE KING AND OTHER STORIES, Rudyard Kipling. 128pp. 28051-9 $1.00

SELECTED SHORT STORIES, D. H. Lawrence. 128pp. 27794-1 $1.00

GREEN TEA AND OTHER GHOST STORIES, J. Sheridan LeFanu. 96pp. 27795-X $1.00

GREAT SPEECHES, Abraham Lincoln. 112pp. 26872-1 $1.00

THE CALL OF THE WILD, Jack London. 64pp. 26472-6 $1.00

FAVORITE POEMS, Henry Wadsworth Longfellow. 96pp. 27273-7 $1.00

THE PRINCE, Niccolò Machiavelli. 80pp. 27274-5 $1.00

BARTLEBY AND BENITO CERENO, Herman Melville. 112pp. 26473-4 $1.00

GREAT SONNETS, Paul Negri (ed.). 96pp. 28052-7 $1.00

SYMPOSIUM AND PHAEDRUS, Plato. 96pp. 27798-4 $1.00

THE TRIAL AND DEATH OF SOCRATES: FOUR DIALOGUES, Plato. 128pp. 27066-1 $1.00

THE GOLD-BUG AND OTHER TALES, Edgar Allan Poe. 128pp. 26875-6 $1.00

THE RAVEN AND OTHER FAVORITE POEMS, Edgar Allan Poe. 64pp. 26685-0 $1.00

ESSAY ON MAN AND OTHER POEMS, Alexander Pope. 128pp. 28053-5 $1.00

THE QUEEN OF SPADES AND OTHER STORIES, Alexander Pushkin. 128pp. 28054-3 $1.00

GOBLIN MARKET AND OTHER POEMS, Christina Rossetti. 64pp. 28055-1 $1.00

CHICAGO POEMS, Carl Sandburg. 80pp. 28057-8 $1.00

COMPLETE SONNETS, William Shakespeare. 80pp. 26686-9 $1.00

HAMLET, William Shakespeare. 128pp. 27278-8 $1.00

KING LEAR, William Shakespeare. 112pp. 28058-6 $1.00

THREE LIVES, Gertrude Stein. 176pp. 28059-4 $2.00

THE STRANGE CASE OF DR. JEKYLL AND MR. HYDE, Robert Louis Stevenson. 64pp. 26688-5 $1.00

THE KREUTZER SONATA AND OTHER SHORT STORIES, Leo Tolstoy. 144pp. 27805-0 $1.00

ADVENTURES OF HUCKLEBERRY FINN, Mark Twain. 224pp. 28061-6 $2.00

THE MYSTERIOUS STRANGER AND OTHER STORIES, Mark Twain. 128pp. 27069-6 $1.00

ETHAN FROME, Edith Wharton. 96pp. 26690-7 $1.00

THE THEORY OF THE LEISURE CLASS, Thorstein Veblen. 256pp. 28062-4 $2.00

CANDIDE, Voltaire. 112pp. 26689-3 $1.00

GREAT LOVE POEMS, Shane Weller (ed.). 128pp. 27284-2 $1.00

SELECTED POEMS, Walt Whitman. 128pp. 26878-0 $1.00

THE IMPORTANCE OF BEING EARNEST, Oscar Wilde. 64pp. 26478-5 $1.00

THE PICTURE OF DORIAN GRAY, Oscar Wilde. 192pp. 27807-7 $1.00

FAVORITE POEMS, William Wordsworth. 80pp. 27073-4 $1.00

EARLY POEMS, William Butler Yeats. 128pp. 27808-5 $1.00

For a complete descriptive list of all volumes in the Dover Thrift Editions series write for a free Dover Fiction and Literature Catalog (59047-X) to Dover Publications, Inc., Dept. DTE, 31 E. 2nd Street, Mineola, NY 11501